An Airman's Wife

An Airman's Wife

A True Story of
Lovers Separated by War

AIMÉE McHARDY

GRUB STREET · LONDON

Published by
Grub Street
4 Rainham Close
London
SW11 6SS

This edition first published in hardback in 2005
Paperback edition 2007

British Library Cataloguing in Publication Data
McHardy, Aimée
  An airman's wife: a true story of lovers separated by war
  1. McHardy, Aimée 2. Bond, William 3. War brides –
  Great Britain – Biography 4. Airmen – Great Britain
  – Biography
  I. Title II. Marsden, Barry
  940.3′0922

ISBN 978-1-904943-94-5

Typeset by Pearl Graphics, Hemel Hempstead

Printed and bound in Great Britain by MPG Ltd, Bodmin, Cornwall

Grub Street only uses FSC (Forest Stewardship Council)
paper for its books.

INTRODUCTION

I first encountered William Arthur Bond—Bill to his friends and relations—when I was researching the stories of Derbyshire fighter pilots in the two World Wars. In a January 1918 issue of the *Derbyshire Times* I came across a full-page review of a book called *An Airman's Wife* by Aimée Bond (neé McHardy) which praised the work as '*so human, so inspiring, that she has done a public service in giving it to the world and by so doing she has raised up a fitting memorial to her husband in the hearts of everyone who reads this book*.' I immediately sought a copy of the work, and found it an inspirational and poignant story, comprised of a collection of letters written by the newly-married Bill Bond to his wife whilst he was on active service, flying Nieuport 17 Scouts with 40 Squadron RFC on the Western Front in the spring and summer of 1917. The book contrasted her own life with that of her husband, and revealed the depth of their mutual feelings and intimacy.

Bill was born in my native town of Chesterfield in June 1889, the eldest son of Arthur and Elizabeth Bond. A keen scholar, he attended St Helen's School, where I myself was later educated, and subsequently won a scholarship to Staveley Netherthorpe Grammar School. He set his sights on becoming a journalist and on leaving school joined the junior staff of the *Huddersfield Examiner*. Eventually he secured a post with the *Daily Mail* and in due course was appointed a sub-editor at the Paris office. Bill undoubtedly lived life to the full and travelled extensively in Europe. He met his long-standing companion and later wife Aimée (elevated by her from the more prosaic Amy) McHardy, of Anglo-Scottish parentage, abroad and the pair indulged in a close and lengthy friendship before their marriage in January 1917.

Aimée was a proto-feminist long before it became fashionable, but without the hard, strident edge of many of her contemporaries. She was a rebel, though I doubt if she would have ever chained herself to any convenient railings, but she had a serene certainty of her worth, and of her enduring love for her husband. Both were authors in their own right, and enjoyed a racy lifestyle which presumably involved living together, and which she described as '*vagabond*', with Bill gaining his colours on the Cresta Run and partaking of idyllic holidays skating and skiing. '*Our outlook is the same*' she wrote '*our work is the same, our desires too... and what one lacks the other seems able to supply.*'

On the outbreak of World War I, Bill volunteered for the armed forces and joined the 20th Hussars. He went to the Dardanelles in July 1915 and was subsequently invalided home from that hell-hole in October. After a period of sick leave he transferred to the 7th Battalion of the King's Own Yorkshire Light Infantry as a 2nd Lieutenant. He won the Military Cross at Ypres in 1916, rescuing a wounded officer from no-man's-land under enemy fire. In the late summer of that year he accepted a new challenge, joining the Royal Flying Corps and living with Aimée in a cottage on Salisbury Plain whilst he was learning to fly at the Central Flying School at nearby Upavon. He gained his 'wings' in November and married Aimée in January 1917 at the St Marylebone Registry Office, near her Oxford Street home. She was vain enough to take a year or two off her age and appear one year younger than her spouse!

In early April, Bill was posted to 40 Squadron RFC, part of the 10th (Army) Wing, and stationed at Treizennes, south-east of St Omer. He was lucky that the unit had just relinquished its clumsy and ineffective FE8 pusher biplanes for the nimble French-built Nieuport 17 Scouts, lively little V-strutted fighters with a good rate of climb. Aimée's book begins with Bill's departure for France, and contrasts her own somewhat simple life in England with his fast-moving and lively existence in the skies above the front-line trenches. The pair wrote prolifically, often despatching several letters a day, and Bill described his combats and general day-to-day doings in great detail, aided by the splendid service provided by the Army postal units. The book itself was of course subjected to heavy censorship, and his fellow pilots were all given pseudonyms in the work. I have managed to provide most of the proper names, and have included them where necessary. Likewise place names were also changed, or replaced by dashes. Where I can locate the originals from the excellent Operations Record Book of the squadron, I have done so.

In her observations, Aimée introduces various personalities; some, like Bill's brother Dick and sister, Joan, are easily identifiable, others are not.

Bill duly became one of the unit's aces, and was

awarded a bar to his MC at the end of May for his *remarkably good and conscientious work* with 40 Squadron. He enjoyed a relaxing leave in early July, and was promoted to the rank of captain and the command of A Flight on his return. Sadly he was shot down by enemy ack-ack on July 22nd, an event which shocked the squadron and had a morale-sapping effect on its pilots. Aimée herself was devastated, and believed for many weeks that her husband might still be alive. When the fact of his death was incontrovertible, she completed her book as some sort of catharsis to enable her to bear the pain of her loss.

I felt from the start that *An Airman's Wife* was a forgotten classic of World War I and was quite frankly amazed that no one had realised its potential before. The book is as readable today as when it was first printed, and fully deserves its resurrection in an up-to-date format. Sadly we know very little of Aimée on a personal basis, and nothing of her life after Bill's death. Likewise his own family left Chesterfield in 1925 and also disappear from the pages of history. I trust however that the story of this brave aviator and his wife will serve to show the calibre of the fighting men produced by this country in the Great War and will help ensure that their endeavours, against a determined and courageous foe, will not fade from the minds of those who benefited so much from their very real sacrifices.

Further, that this immensely powerful love story will live on forever.

Barry M. Marsden,
Eldwick 2007

AN AIRMAN'S WIFE

I

ON Wednesday, very early in the morning, Bill went to France.

"Can't I go too—to Folkestone, I mean?" I said to the officer person who stood just inside the platform gates beside a sort of desk where they all had to sign their names.

"I'm sorry—if you were the wife of a Brigadier-General you couldn't," he replied very kindly, adding, "One tried last week, and she was brought back under arrest."

I smiled back at him, but I had to bite my lip.

Bill appeared just then. He had been seeing about his baggage and things.

"Have you asked?" he questioned, and his face was quite solid.

"Yes, ... I can't come," I told him.

We walked along the platform. It was busy with those who were going, like Bill; and those who were being left behind, like me.

There were a few moments only. We stood

by the carriage door and didn't say anything.
I felt I couldn't begin because there would be
no time to finish. I daresay Bill felt the same.

Anyway my throat was funny and I didn't
want him to know.

They began to bang the doors. Suddenly I
had to speak. It was urgent.

"Don't kiss me here," I whispered in a panic;
but after all he couldn't have heard, for he bent
down.

"If the boat is delayed I'll wire and you'll
come at once, won't you?" he said, and kissed
my mouth.

I nodded my head: the train moved.

"Good-bye, old boy," I managed quite
clearly, and smiled.

He smiled too.

"Good-bye," he said.

I don't know if he hung out of the window,
for I walked away and never looked round.
Outside, although it was spring-time, the rain
and the snow came down together.

I wondered what to do, and as it didn't seem
to matter much I got into the 'bus that no one
appeared to want. When it had been going for
some time, I got out and went in an Under-
ground.

Then I remembered that I'd left all our
luggage at the hotel.

"But I'll go home first, though," I thought.

'Home' meant the place I lived in before I married Bill. No one bothers about you there. You can stow yourself away and arrange all your thoughts for as long as you like—that is if you can find an empty place.

When Purcell opened the door she looked surprised first, then understood.

"Oh, miss, has he gone?" she said.

"Yes," I answered, and ran upstairs as fast as I could.

In my old room the gramophone lay on a table and I recalled how Bill had wound it up the night we slept there. It was when we came to town unexpectedly once and couldn't get in at the hotel where we stay for sentimental reasons that wouldn't appeal to anyone but ourselves.

We had danced to a ragtime tune—he in his blue crêpe-de-chine pyjamas and me in the state of undress that makes him call me his "Kirchner" girl. Now I put on the same record and watched it while it solidly ground away. Just as it finished with a horrid scrape, and I was wondering what to do to make it stop, Purcell came in with a tray, holding steaming coffee, and bread and honey and the morning newspaper.

"There you are, miss," she said, placing it on another small table and dragging it over to the fire to which she set a match.

I don't know whether it was her tone, or the scent of the coffee, or the sight of the newspaper, or the crackle of the flames—but all at once something cleared away the cloud that had swallowed me up ever since the night before when Bill had come back from Adastral House and announced:

"They won't give any leave—I am to go in the morning."

Those words had bothered me ever since, but now I remembered something else.

In the night he had spoken.

"You must be happy," he had said. "I'll come back to you, I know.... All our life together, our wonderful adventures and our work... all is so clearly mapped out... I feel I'm coming back to you... You're to be happy."

"Yes," I answered—whispered, you know, like you do in bed because your faces are close to each others. There was a pause. I knew something waited. I scarcely breathed, and it came at last.

"And if I shouldn't come," ...he went on. ..."If I shouldn't come, you're to be happy even then," he said.

II

AND I *have* been happy—ever since.

It is as though a presence is with me; the embodiment perhaps of Bill's philosophy.

He believes, you know, that we make our own light or darkness as we go, and his refusal to be baffled by circumstance is not merely the outcome of good health and a man's more sweeping outlook, as I told myself at first it must be.

Now, sometimes, I wonder at my calm. I wonder how other wives feel, and I recall some I have known during these years of war. Those who have loved their men have been feverish all the while—aching with loneliness—adrift—forlorn.

In spite of work, or perhaps because the labour they have chosen has been too strenuous or too unusual, their health seems to have suffered; and husbands, returning, have found what I think soldier men have no right to expect—wives more in need of doctors than husbands.

And so I—who have rebelled always, who

have, until now, refused to accept even the inevitable—am glad of, while I marvel at, my calm.

The first letter was written before he crossed. I knew it was meant just to greet me when I wakened because he would not be with me to kiss before we spoke.

When Purcell had gone, with my head still on the pillow, I read:

"Ma Bien Aimée,

I discovered that, because I was 'O.C. train,' I had to wait for the second boat.

Immediately I looked up the guide but found you could not reach me before it left.

It will be a very rough crossing—a sort of switch-back one that would make you giddy even to contemplate.

I hope you are feeling as cheery as I am. I find myself in excellent spirits— not excited, you know, but buoyed up by interest.

I am longing to know my address though, so that I can begin to hear from you.

All my love, my darling wife,

BILL."

I pressed my face against the join of the

pillows, for that is where our lips always met instinctively almost before sleep had unclosed our eyes.

At lunch time a telegram came from France, giving the address, so that immediately after I was able to send all that I'd talked of on paper since he went. Then I had to wait until Saturday morning for all that he had spoken on Thursday.

Doesn't it seem absurd—and yet so amazing! This is what he said:

"My darling wife,

My luck's all in as usual, for I have come to one of the best squadrons in a good part of the line. The machines are things of beauty and the mess is splendid. What more could a flying man want? I am to fly a —— scout, which is, if anything, better than the one I flew at home. They dive faster and fly and climb quite as well.

You'd go into an ecstacy if you saw one.

I am longing to try one, but shall have to wait a day or two when I shall have a new one: all mine, like you.

The weather is very wild and there is little doing.

I reached here last night. On landing I was put on a tender and had a three hours' ride over the hills through the rain.

And when I went to the orderly room to report I found myself reporting to Hyatt. I was awfully pleased. He arrived four days ago. It's great luck, I think, and further, I've been posted to the same flight.

I know lots of the fellows here; for on the same aerodrome is the squadron to which FitzGarrick came; but I learn that he went down behind the Hun lines a few days ago—under control, so it is presumed that he is a prisoner. Engine failure must have caused it.

I'm sorry I took such trouble to keep down my kit, for travelling was so easy that I could have brought three times as much.

But I can't think of anything I want you to send me except your letters and your love.

It is so much sweeter to be out here knowing that I have someone who matters so enormously to me. I am very happy, ma bien Aimée.

When I was in the train and leaving London I thought for the first time of your precious tears. It thrilled me, darling, to think of them—to remember you lying in my arms making my face all wet.

I realized that I couldn't realize how much I love you.

Darling wife, I am so glad you wept in my arms. I treasure the memory of it intensely.

All my love,

BILL.

P.S.—I came across a topping book at Folkestone—a quaint yarn about the Latin quarter—by a young Canadian officer, who also has written some quite good verse.

It's 'racy' and therefore not flawless, but his pictures of the quarter are lovely, I think.

By the way, my next letter will be addressed to the country, for I don't want to think of you in town."

Isn't it remarkable! Hyatt and Bill were at Sulva together and, later, in the trenches in France, where each won his "little bit of ribbon." Then, when both volunteered for the Corps, they met on the same aerodrome in England; and both, having married in the same week, brought wives who called each of them "Bill" to the same cottage on the edge of Salisbury Plain—All by chance—without pre-arrangement!

The wives were different though. Hyatt chose a lovely woman—fair and with delicious features. Her blue eyes gazed from dark lashes too, and her brows were dark.

Usually I can admire impersonally, but after looking at her I said to Bill:

"I wish I were beautiful also."

He turned from the glass where the important business of hair-brushing was taking place. His tone was awfully serious.

"You're not to wish that—You mustn't wish that—Tell me you don't wish it," he said.

"I don't wish it," I answered, "but why?"

"Because we're so happy—so content... Because I love your face just as it is... I wouldn't have it altered the tiniest little bit!"

Isn't he rather satisfactory?

It was amusing to talk to the other Mrs. Bill. She and her man looked forward to a house in Kensington or Hampstead and they had the furniture all arranged. She was sorry for me, I think, when I told her we don't mean to have a house at all because we want to explore so much of the world.

Soon I realized that we spoke a different language, so I didn't say much about the Studio in the Quartier Latin, or the cottage of Madame Champigny on the Seine, or our winters in Switzerland where the hot sun glints on the snow.

She is no vagabond—the other Mrs. Bill— but she has a lovely face.

III

An old man is cutting the hedge. Every minute he takes several steps backward and stares at what he has done.

The air is soft and damp from yesterday's rain, but the sky is blue except for the fluffiest white eiderdown clouds.

I wonder if the sky is blue in France?

The old man who cuts the hedge has three there—one buried: one in hospital: and one in the big new Advance.

I daresay his thoughts are with them when he steps backward and stares, instead of with the bare places from which the branches have been clipped.

Most of the garden we attend to ourselves. I'm the "handy Andy" one. You remember how, at the circus, he always trod on everything and got in everyone's way! A row of peas and one bean have peeped out of the earth.

Molly fills me with wonderment. Before breakfast she grooms Joey; and if anything goes wrong with Polly Blue she just takes off her bonnet and pulls her engine to bits—and puts it together again.

Then, without neglecting the family in the least, she writes an article on a topical subject just at the most topical moment; and in the evening she looks as feminine as a woman who has done nothing except care for herself all day.

Besides all this she interests herself in the welfare of the village, and when the tractor plough has convalesced she means to help to plough the fields.

In addition to this the most important lady of the County called on Tuesday to suggest that she also might undertake the job of Agricultural Registrar, as the vicar doesn't seem too enthusiastic about the work. Molly pointed out that the need is small in a village like this, where the few women there are labour on the land of their own accord—of necessity, you know, to take the place of their men; but if, as a matter of form, it has to be done, so that every village is accounted for, she will add that to her routine and never turn a hair.

As for me—it takes me all my time to get up and to do my exercises and dress before my tray comes.

Molly likes to breakfast alone with her family; and so I, with my casement window opened wide, may eat my porridge looking beyond the trees of the garden and the dull red roofs of the barns, and beyond the windmill too, on to the Downs from which comes the breath of a far-off sea.

And I have my letter from Bill to read!

No wonder I feel content.

Of course some there are who think it unbecoming to be happy now when so many suffer and are sad, but I say that there is enough sorrow. I, too, have had some and imagined more, but now I will be glad while I may; and if it should happen that sorrow comes again I hope I still shall have courage to be glad.

My letter on Monday said:

"Bien Aimée,

This morning I made my first trip on this machine.

It was quite successful, and I found it, if anything, easier to take off the ground and to land than the one at home; but it was very different in the air, much heavier and trickier on the steep turns.

I did two spins but did not loop. Then later I went up again for machine-gun practice, which consists of diving at a target on the ground and firing at it.

The weather has been very much better today, though now it is getting squally again.

But I'm forgetting the news. Hyatt went over the lines on patrol this morning for the first time and got a Hun!

It was quite comical too. He was out with two others and when over the lines got lost in the clouds. He searched around for some time, not knowing at all where he was, and then suddenly a Hun two-seater came out of a cloud and flew at him. Hyatt fired promptly and saw the Hun turn over, go down spinning and crash to the ground.

Then he got 'Archied' and climbed out of it, guessed his way and landed an hour overdue.

How are you? I send all my love,

BILL."

As I owed the other Mrs. Bill a letter, after breakfast I wrote to tell her the news in case her husband, man-like, forgot to mention it. But I know her pleasure at his feat will be counter-balanced, as mine would be, by the thought that some woman suffers through it.

Later we tramped through the fields and into the woods.

An old man worked in a clearing making hurdles. The sun, unwilling that day for the rest of us, was pleased to shine on him. Tall and erect he stood. His earth-stained clothes seemed a part of him and he seemed a part of the land.

Gaiters held together by string, corduroy

breeches whose patches even had worn through, a coat out at elbows and a ragged cowboy hat over his tawny hair—such clothes in town would seem inadequate, but here, where the dirt is Nature's own, they made the picture more complete.

A pile of hurdles were stacked; another was being added to with easy speed. A blade, strong-handled, an upright block, and a curved bar upon the ground, were all the tools he used as he cut and split and bent the supple wood.

On we went—Molly and I and her family of one, for Nanny chose to be busy at home and Joey ran wild in his field.

Garry spied the primroses first and the violets too, but for the daffodils we hunted in vain.

IV

IN today's paper there is an account of a divorce case.

Both letters are dignified. The happiness they gave to one another; the years of congenial work together; the understanding and sympathy, are not denied. Each is grateful to the other, but, as the man says, "Things change!"

Now this is a prospect Bill and I have discussed. It comes as a shock, in the midst of perfect agreement, to recall that nothing remains just as it is; that two human beings seldom develop equally; that chance may bring another woman—another man.

In reason can one hope to be more than a very precious part of another's sum total of living?

Bill and I have made no vows to one another beyond the formal words spoken at the marriage office.

Yet we set out with brighter prospects than most. Our outlook is the same, our work is the same, our desires too, for both are vagabonds! And what one lacks the other seems able to supply. Indeed our chances are fair—yet we have made no vows.

Tuesday's letter said:

"Ma Bien Aimée,
    To-night I hope to get your first letter —Darling?
    I did no more flying yesterday than the two trips I told you of. In the evening, rather to my surprise, I was told to go out on a line patrol with two others. I was very pleased because it was a perfect evening, and I should have got a good idea of the line without going over it.

However, when we were already in the machines it was all washed out, and the others—the experienced ones—were sent to convoy a bombing raid.

This morning, however, I was put on the first offensive patrol and went over with two others.

I thoroughly enjoyed it. We started at 6.45 in triangular formation and worked down on our side of the line, crossed it at 12,000 feet, and worked back north about eight miles the other side. We saw five Hun machines which kept a long way clear and were 'Archied' nearly all the time. I saw a good deal of the line though I was busy mostly trying to keep my place in the formation.

We were out one hour and forty-five minutes, and I was told that I had flown quite well. And so to breakfast.

Have you any of my towels? I need another as I brought only two. Another khaki shirt too, if you please.

The weather is very fine but rough.

All my love,

BILL."

I'm sure I don't know where the towels are—or the shirt.

The only shirt I have is the one his mother

sent to Suvla. Thinking it a happy inspiration she gathered some apples from the garden and wrapped them in it, and when, after months of travel to the Dardanelles and back again, the parcel came to be opened it simply knocked them down.

The apples were no more, and the tail of the shirt had rotted into holes.

After it had been scalded and had hung out in the air for days, Bill—home on sick leave— commandeered it for a relic. He wore it on his marriage day—holes and all.

We're rather fond of that shirt.

But I must write to town and order what he needs.

I'm sure he must have gone without lots of things, for his packing appears to be the most casual affair.

Smokes and hair lotion seem to be the only things that matter; and I'm afraid I like too much to sit and watch him mix tobacco on a newspaper to do my wifely bit.

Besides I don't want to get into a habit of bothering him with small enquiries. I think wives begin to be a burden when they go into detail too much.

Wednesday's letter was simply a scrawl to say that nothing had arrived from me. It was written on Sunday and my first letter was posted from town on Thursday afternoon, so I

suppose the boat must have been delayed.
Thursday brought a lovely budget though.

"Darling,

At last I have your letters (he wrote).
There are two of them, the first two. It is
so thrilling to hear about you. By this
time you will have had several letters
from me, so many of your questions are
answered.

To what I have told you I can only add
that I am more than content to be in this
squadron. There are some awfully good
fellows in it: good fellows both as pilots
and personally.

My flight commander, Captain Romney,
came out eight months ago and is a great
Hun Strafer. Several years before the war
he was an art student in the Quartier.

He leads our patrol, and I need not
assure you how closely I hang on to his tail.
We have tremendous confidence in him.

Incidentally he formed a good opinion
of me, which may explain why he took
me over the lines so soon.

To-day is a 'dud' day, so everything is
washed out. The same thing happened
yesterday afternoon, but I was up for
fifteen minutes in the gale to try my new
machine. It is splendid. It climbed

incredibly fast and flew level at a topping speed.

All the gun fittings are being finished to-day, and to-morrow I shall take it over the lines.

I haven't said much about going over the lines—about my impressions, I mean. Well, really, I didn't have any very pronounced ones. The principal thing I felt was that comical sort of detachment I have had in other things—as if someone else were doing the show and I were looking on. But I was elated to be so high above the clouds looking down through the holes on towns and villages eight or ten miles behind the German lines.

It was thrilling but not exciting. It was thrilling to be all alone in my machine, depending on myself and good luck. (I'm thankful I'm not responsible for an observer.) And yet I could not help being astonished at the absolute absence of emotion—no anxiety, no fear, no care— except one, to stick close to the patrol leader.

As we were crossing the lines initially we had one burst of anti-aircraft shells put up against us, but it was very wide and we did not change our course. The German A.-A. shells burst in black woolly balls and they generally put up about a dozen all around one at once.

I told you I could hear nothing in the air. I was wrong. I can hear 'Archie' bursts when they are near me. The noise is curious. Something like: 'Woof! Brupp!' and if the burst is quite near the machine rocks about.

On our return, however, while we were over 15,000, the Boche gunners got us very well, and then for ten minutes we dived and zoomed to throw his ranging out and came through untouched.

Then the leader dived into the clouds, which had gathered thickly and risen to the height of about 9,000 feet. After him we all dived, and then for nearly five minutes I saw nothing but thick fog all round me. I looked frequently at my Pitot, which was registering a steady 120 miles an hour, and kept hoping I wouldn't run into the leader or into Hyatt, who was just on my right.

At last I came out at about 3,000 feet and just over our side of the trenches; and, looking round, found the formation about 500 yards away on my right. Except for being more widely apart than when we started we were still in formation.

With the mail, bringing your letters,

came my new tunic and breeches. They are topping. I wish you could see them. The stream-line cap is quite all right too.

Yesterday afternoon, after testing my 'bus, I went out for a ride with Hyatt. I struck a quite lively mount who tried hard for ten minutes to get rid of me before he yielded to coercion. Then my stirrup leather broke and I had to return.

As the weather is so bad to-day we may have a tender to go to the Vimy ridge for a look round the captured trenches.

Darling wife, I have so many sweet souvenirs of you in my mind. I am loving you just all the time.

BILL."

V

TO-DAY no letter has come from my love. I want one. I want him to fly over the edge of the Downs and in at my bedroom window. I want to kiss his mouth.

Molly has taken her family to find chalk to burn on the fire.

Miss Kerr-Kerr told us about it yesterday when she came to tea. You put a few lumps on with the coal and apparently it stays red-hot. We hope it does, for the coal-cellar is getting rather empty and no one for miles around seems to have any to supply.

Thank goodness the summer is coming and not a long chilly winter like the one that is loth to leave us now.

To-day we feel dissipated. Last night a concert was held at the next village inn and we sat for three hours without ventilation, breathing hot humanity.

The village children, wearing their starched white frocks with bright blue and pink ribbons, did nursery rhymes and tableaux.

Their faces shone and their hands, too, and their hair was crimped until it stuck out from their heads.

We had a song, about the boys coming home, by a very thin woman with a very large mouth; and another song, about a diver who slept at the bottom of the sea, by a third of the old men who seem to blossom here. He twitched a lot, but valiantly went through it twice like every-one else.

Then came revue songs of the season before last and one doubtful joke by an experienced labourer of sixteen.

There were piano solos and dialogues and a speech by the preacher man, who has here such a priceless opportunity for simplicity.

At ten o'clock we came out into the clean night air, glancing, now and then, as we strolled along, into the ditch on either side of the road; for Nanny, having driven us in Polly Blue backed up by Molly's support, had raced back home alone.

The most unforeseen things happen to Polly's mechanism, but somehow she manages always to do what is asked of her. We found Nanny in the Nursery, and there was a jug of hot coffee in the grate. We sat round on low stools and drank while we told each other all the news.

VI

THIS morning when Mabel pulled back the chintz curtains from my casement window the brightest day poured in. It was all so fresh and clean that I might have been wakened out of doors. Then later when my breakfast tray came up, on it were two letters and a book from France.

Is it any wonder that I paid no attention whatever to the long envelope!

The writing of the returned pot-boiler it contained had amused *us* for an evening in our cottage parlour on the slope of Salisbury Plain—so it had served its turn.

Yesterday's letter was short—just a note to say that two only of mine had reached my Bill, so today's I opened avariciously to read that still no more news had found its way to him.

But he understands that the post, not I, is to blame.

"Ma Bien Aimée," he says,

"There has been no mail again since the day before yesterday (Tuesday), but I hope to hear from you to-day.

The mail is much worse than it used to be; it is taking a minimum of four days to get a letter from home now.

Yesterday afternoon I went with Hyatt on a tender to S—— and had a bath—a very hot one. I wished you were there to have it first, as you used to in the country when the hot water was too precious to be wasted on one.

This morning I was out on early patrol with Hyatt and another fellow. We were across the lines at 7 a.m., but saw nothing. The clouds had gathered below us and we finished our patrol flying over the trenches at 1,000 feet.

After breakfast I was up for half an hour on target practice.

A remarkable incident happened just after I came down. Another fellow on target practice was diving vertically at the target from 1,500 feet when his right-hand lower wing came off. He heeled over to the right but managed to get her level with his aileron controls, shut off his engine and glided down slowly and crashed in a ploughed field without being hurt. It was a splendid effort. I saw the whole thing happen.

I haven't done any work. I'm busy reading 'The Opium Eater.'

Yesterday, though, I did a cheap parody on the 'jabberwock.' A few days ago one of the much despised quirks brought down a new fast Hun scout: quite to our disgust. Voila—'The Jabberwock and the Quirk.'

'Twas brillig and the Slithy Quirk
Did drone and burble in the blue,
All floppy were his wing controls
(And his Observer too).

'Beware the wicked Albatross,'
The 'O.C. quirks' had told him flat;
'Beware the Hun-Hun bird and shun
'The frumious Halberstadt.'

But while through uffish bumps he ploughed,
The Albatross, with tail on high,
Came diving out the tulgey cloud
And let his bullets fly.

One, two; one, two, and through and through,
The Lewis gun went tick-a-tack,
The Hun was floored, the Quirk had scored,
And me galumpling back.

'Oh, hast thou slain the Albatross?
'Split one, with me, my beamish boy,
'Our R.A.F.'-ish scout has found them out.'
The C.O. wept for joy.'

(R.A.F.-Royal Aircraft Factory.)

You'll find, if it's worth looking at so closely, that the system of rhyming isn't regular, but neither is it in the original.

After Lunch.
"I have just got your note written on Sunday morning!

By the same post came one from mother. She gives me tons of good advice. She says: 'Be calm, careful and contented, and last, but not least, steady!' Oh, Fids! isn't she delicious!

All my love, darling,

BILL."

I think Bill and I are especially lucky in our choice of mothers.

Sometimes you scarcely could believe that anyone living on this planet should remain so unwordly as Bill's mother, but he vows she has a little spice of "La Diable" (the French one) in her veins. It has been discouraged, of course—by Dad and her environment; but it's there and shows itself in a few saucy ways.

"I get it all from her," Bill said once, and of course *I* understood what he meant—but *she* wouldn't!

The other letter, which had been opened by the base censor, had been posted three days before. The brand new machine he speaks of must be the same he wrote of since in the letter that came several days ago. But here is the whole:

"Ma Bien Aimée,

I did a big escort and patrol this morning. There were seven of us escorting six two-seater machines and we went about ten miles over the lines at 15,000 feet. I found that the height didn't affect me in the least.

A brand new machine has just arrived for me and is being fitted for a trial test this afternoon.

By the way, I forgot to tell you more about FitzGarrick. I asked particularly how he got on out here, and was told that the FitzGarrick here was entirely different from the FitzGarrick at the home aerodrome. He was much more lively and agreeable in mess and quite eager and steady as a pilot. Incidentally he was called 'Iolanthe.'

I am still waiting to hear from you. The post has been very much delayed, during the present push.

Poor Cotton, who is in the other squadron on our aerodrome, looks very miserable. I feel I ought to conceal my own good spirits when I talk to him. You see he crashed so many scouts at home that he was sent out on a two-seater and he doesn't like it all.

All my love, ma bébé,

BILL."

The book was "The Pretender," by Robert W. Service. I shall read it in bed to-night, for now Molly and I and her family of one are going on to the Downs to catch the sun and play with the wind.

I forgot to tell you that we went to church—except Molly who stayed to finish an article. I disgraced myself several times. First of all I went without my collection and had to run back, then I led Garry into the wrong pew, and we followed thinking "The Aunt" could do no wrong.

When we had been hauled out by Nanny and things had gone smoothly for a while I knocked

Garry's penny out of his hand as we both tried to reach the bag at the same moment.

Then to prove that we don't always get our deserts a most unexpected release occurred.

The family and Nanny having disappeared discreetly during the end of the hymn, I had collected all the prayer mats together with my feet preparatory to listening to "Horace's" oration in comparative comfort, when the whole thing was, as Bill would say, "washed out."

That happens sometimes. You have something tacked on to service and you do without a sermon. My joy was improper. I hastened home to my writing table, but paused on the way to have a word with the old lady at whose house we drank tea some days ago.

Her head nods all the time as though it were fixed to a spring, and her eyes must be as old as the pyramids.

I wonder what thoughts pass through her brain.

VII

"My wife—dearest,

I'm so happy to read of your contentment and comfort. I have just got your letter—the first real one from the country—telling me of your room into which I fit so unobtrusively.

By the same post I had a letter from Cox's saying they have sent you a cheque book. They did not tell me how my account stood. When I left there wasn't much in credit, but there were many payments overdue, and when I am gazetted there will be 8/6 a day in arrear from last month, to go in. However, in any case I shall not be drawing on the account until about the end of the month, so any small cheques you draw will be all right.

I was over the lines for about two hours this morning. We went out at 7 a.m. and saw nothing. This afternoon Hyatt and I may get permission to fly over to another squadron to see various people.

I have forgotten to mention that my ideas of saving have been modified slightly. I told you it was a good mess— really it is much more; it is a wonderful mess. But it is not cheap. However, I don't complain a scrap because it is so lovely to have the comfort and excellent food on active service.

That's all. Remember me, please, to Molly and Garry.

All my love.

BILL."

Neither do I complain a scrap.

"My gracious no!" as Madame used to say.

Indeed I find it is most essential to a wife to know that her man is well nourished, otherwise the maternal instinct would be perplexed dreadfully.

They amused Bill—my spasms of looking after him.

Once, when he was springing from a taxi, carelessly, before it had stopped, I cried: "Be careful."

"I've been doing it for quite a number of years," he said as he held out his hand to help me—and we both laughed.

Yet they love to be spoiled—just enough and not too much—but that's the secret of everything, isn't it? Just enough and not too much.

To-day on our way through the fields up to the Downs we met old Witchell, wearing his best black clothes and a new pale green satin spotted tie.

"That's to show he's on his club, and for the time being not a working man," explained Molly in an undertone.

"And how's your lumbago to-day, Witchell?" she asked aloud.

"Not so bad and not so good," he beamed, his round, red face creased with smiles—"and how be you, Master Garry?" he added, looking down upon the small shrimp who gazed up with wide eyes.

"Ve'ey well, fank you, Wit-fel—an' how be Jack and Jim?"

With this opening old Witchell began. Many times already had Garry heard the recital of Jack, who is with the Marines; and of Jim, who has been with his battalion in the East "these two year past cum May," but the spratling, all eagerness, breathed it in once more; for he is of that priceless specie—the ardent listener.

"And you be goin' to be a sailor lad yourself, Master Garry—maybe an Admiral an' all!" finished the old man at length.

"Yeth—I do be," agreed Garry blandly, taking his rank as a matter of course.

Then it was that the so unreasonable momentary depression came down upon me.

Perhaps Molly felt it too. Garry an Admiral! By that day old Witchell would have gone: by that time Witchell's sons and Molly and I would be as old as he is now; and the small spratling whose small tongue can't yet command his words would have seen much water; would have sailed far from his world, bounded now by the tall hedge that hides it from the road.

Indeed things change!

But have we learned anything at all if that truth hurts us one little bit? Mon Dieu, we unlearn our lessons as fast as we take them in!

On and upward we tramped—our Admiral keeping pace; and soon, high on the level of the Downs, we came to the sign of a more immediate change.

"Those are the jumps Curtis spoke of—you remember?" Molly said.

My thoughts retraced themselves to an afternoon last week when walking to "Rutham's Folly"—that weird tower on the hill on the other side of the Vale—we came across a woman who, till then, I had thought of only as the manipulator of the harmonium in the village church. Soon it was arranged that we should go back to the farm for tea.

There the pictures first attracted my attention. They were a queer mixture—old prints—sets of them—mellow and quaintly designed; and beside them crude modern pages torn from journals, and drawings and etchings and paintings in oil and wash. One and all included those long sleek horses that seem to slip through the air rather than run on legs.

Round the parlour table—eating maize bread and home-made butter and drinking cup after cup of tea—I began to comprehend. The talk, too, was of horses and nothing else. Even the war was mentioned from their point of view: races were rerun and each animal was spoken of as though it were a loved child—since gone out into the world.

"Prince now—that day he walked his eighteen miles to the course; won his two races and walked all the way home again, for he didn't like to sleep away from his bed. Once there, though, he lay down and for the first time in his life admitted he was tired."

As he spoke the meagre young old man gazed at each of us in turn. Molly rose to the occasion.

"A wonderful horse!" she said.

"Yes, and he had the pluck of twelve, had old Prince—the beauty. You should have seen him take those jumps on the Downs! His grave is out there in the field—a proper one he has!"

The Harmonium lady spoke with wistful tears in her eyes, and even I understood.

These were people I never before had come in contact with. Somehow I had thought of them as gamblers only; but now I realized that they had lived *for* their horses rather than *by* them.

War has changed their mode of life, and agriculture and farm produce now occupy their time. The steeplechasers are scattered, the riders scattered too—and the unused jumps on the Downs stand as monuments.

VIII

"MA Bien Aimée,

After the big budget of yesterday I had only one letter this morning—from father. Mother enclosed a note in which she addresses me as 'My dear Boy,' the result, I suppose, of your rallying her. You remember how we puzzled about her meaning in the letter that came on our marriage day, 'My dear Boy—I suppose this is the last time I can call you that——!'

If she's not careful she will provoke me into marrying you again or doing something reckless.

After writing to you yesterday I was sent up at 6.30, and during an hour and a half we saw one Hun. This morning we did not see any. I suppose I'll come across swarms at once. I expect there will be much more doing shortly. To-day it is cloudy, but one can get up through the gaps and it is perfectly clear above.

Last night I lay awake a long time thinking of you. It was so wonderfully sweet.

My darling wife, I love you.

All yours,

BILL."

I am so glad I am his wife: I am so glad he stayed awake in the night thinking of me: and that the thought of me is sweet.

But women have to be made of wood and iron now-a-days, I think.

Listen to this:

"Darling,

I told you that when we did see Huns, we'd see a whole lot. We did!

Our repeated failure to see them was annoying, as other patrols came in and reported the sky thick with them. Messages came from the infantry and artillery stating that Huns were about in hundreds.

But our patrol—Duff, leader; Hyatt on the left, and Your Husband on the right—never saw one within ten miles and just said so. The temptation to see them at all costs was growing, however, and when we were getting ready to start again last night—Sunday evening—Duff said:

'It's no use; we've just *got* to see Huns, so take it from me we're going to see five at least—in our report!'

So we crossed the lines 8,000 feet and climbed steadily, going due east. For nearly half an hour we had the sky to ourselves; then we saw Duff whip round to the left and dive. Looking down in his direction, we saw Huns. Real Huns! Four big, fat ones!

Two were painted a vivid red; the others were a nasty mottled yellow and green. But we didn't mind. They could have had puce hair and scarlet eyes, for all we cared.

Now, when you're on patrol and the leader dives on a Hun, the other scouts have to search the sky above and behind them for other Huns before following. It is a favourite trick of the Boche to plant a couple of machines below you as bait, and then wait above until you go down. Then they dive on you when your attention is occupied.

Neither Hyatt nor I overlooked this, and before we had dived far we saw that this had happened. Five Huns were on our tail!

We opened out, and went past Duff. Duff looked round and saw the Huns, and started to climb dead into the sun and forward the five.

They turned off at this, and passed us about 2,000 yards away.

We continued to climb and circle, so that we got the sun behind us.

Then we began to see Huns in earnest. From every one of the 360 degrees of the compass they came. Still we climbed and circled, waiting for their attack. Gradually they gathered together, until we could count fourteen. Some could outclimb us we could see; but they stayed together, and when we were as high as they, Duff headed straight for them.

Immediately they split into parties, left and right; while two dived underneath us. This was the bait trick again, and we refused it. Again we circled back into the sun and awaited their attack. It never came; but all the time the west wind was drifting us further over Hun land.

The finish was a comedy. Duff made a quick left turn, and Hyatt, on the inside, tried a vertical bank; but so absorbed was he in watching the rainbow formation in front of us that he turned right over and went down in a spin. I thought, perhaps, he had been hit, and looked behind. Three more Huns on our tail!

Hyatt had gone right down into the clouds. I looked for Duff, and could not see him. I was alone against the whole Hunnish Flying Corps!

.   .   .   .

When I stopped spinning, I was just above the clouds at 7,000 feet. My spin had started at 13,000.

I headed carefully for the sun, due west, and home. Then I looked back. The Huns were still there—just a few dots in infinite distance.

Sometime afterwards I picked up Hyatt, and together we tootled home. Duff landed a few minutes later.

In our report we mentioned that we had seen *a* Hun!

I find the pen excellent. Thanks. Your letter of Thursday has just arrived.

All my love, dearest,

BILL.

P.S.—This morning we went out and saw another Hun—and got him. Will tell you about it to-night. Just going out again."

IX

MY breakfast tray has come. On it, in blue and white cottage china, are porridge and coffee and some home-made maize cakes that are eaten with syrup.

These things are pleasant to contemplate but the pleasantest of all is my letter with the post mark, "Passed Field Censor."

It is a thick budget that I tear open and read:

"My Bien Aimée,

To continue the tale of ourselves and the Huns:—

Neither Hyatt nor Duff nor I were feeling absolutely full of confidence, nor pleased with life, last night. The idea of Huns jostling each other in the sky like that was not nice to think about. Hyatt and I thought we'd dream of Huns—pink ones and red and green—but we didn't.

This morning I started right away to get back my confidence by going up after breakfast for half an hour's joy-ride. I climbed to 7,000, and then looped three times, did about a dozen violent vertical bank turns left and right, a vertical spiral, and a spinning nose dive of 2,000 feet. I felt enormously better for it.

At 11 a.m. we went over the lines. We crossed at 9,000, and almost immediately saw one Hun. With last night fresh in our minds we looked for the others, but they were not there. It seemed too easy.

When we first saw him we were above him and a long way to his north—all going east. We climbed behind him, and got right round to the east of him and dived. Duff fired first and passed under him, and I then went all out for him. I got him dead in the sights, and when less than 100 yards away I fired. One shot answered, and then the gun stopped. I sheered away and climbed, trying desperately to clear the gun which had jammed. I cocked it as I thought, and went in again down on his tail. At not more than 50 yards' range I fired again—at least I pulled the lever—but nothing happened. Still sighting dead on, I cocked the gun twice more. It was hopelessly jammed.

The Hun had turned on me now. I spun in the approved C.F.S. way. When I turned level, Hyatt was diving on him and I saw him going down, turning over slowly until he fell into the clouds.

We came home fearfully bucked; but I pulled down my gun—it is mounted over the top plane above my head—and found a hellish jam. I blasphemed and yelled to myself all alone!

It was just this I was going to tell you about just before going out, but there was no time.

This morning's exploit was eclipsed this afternoon.

We went out in the same way, and after going about 5 miles over the lines turned and spotted two Huns about 2,000 feet below us. Duff dived on one and I on the other. I went down nearly vertically, sighting on. (Incidentally I glanced at the Pitot, which was showing 160 miles an hour.)

I fired a burst at 150 yards' range and felt sure I had hit the machine near the observer's seat. I passed right underneath him, pulled up quickly, turned, and found myself facing him broadside on. I fired two more bursts. I wondered why the observer did not fire at me, and concluded I had put him out.

Then my gun stopped, and at the same moment the Hun turned and got his forward gun on me. I heard and thought I saw about 20 shots come my way and decided it was enough. Out came the spinning trick once more, and when I came out and looked round, the sky was bare.

The rest of the story I learned on the aerodrome. Hyatt and Duff landed ten minutes after me.

Hyatt had been watching me tackling my Hun, and when I suddenly sheered off he saw the Hun dive also. Hyatt followed him down nearly 5,000 feet through the clouds and fired a burst at him. Then he found himself 800 feet off the ground and decided to leave it at that, and climbed above the clouds again and came home. He, too, thought that the observer must have been done in as he (Hyatt) was not fired on.

Duff's experience was different. After getting off one short burst at his Hun he turned round just in time to see another Hun dive past him firing, and three others above him.

So he came home!

Half an hour later the Artillery people reported that a Hun two-seater had nose-dived through the clouds and was believed to have crashed. Our Hun!

If my gun hadn't jammed this morning I'd have had one off my own bat. However our patrol—which simply couldn't see a Hun before—has driven two down to-day.

Your letters are so sweet. I do love you. I got your lovely long one of the 19th just after I got back this morning. It was so perfect to read what you are doing and to know you're so happy. I, too, am very happy—in the knowledge of your love for me and mine for you; it is still quite wonderful; more wonderful, in fact, every day. Darling Aimée, all my wife. (I like writing it.)

Well, about the book; Molly's criticism of the diary used as it is, was mine, you will recall: I thought it abrupt, too. Besides, it is called 'Ad Astra'; and the Suvla and Ypres diary *have* nothing to do with my being an airman. However, I agree with your idea of trying it as it is, and in the meantime I may develop some material for its reconstruction, to fit the title idea better.

All my love,

BILL."

X

FROM where I sit in the garden under the trees I can see the ridge of the Downs against the sky—and all is radiant with sunshine.

I think of my Love, and my heart is full of joy because he is mine. He is like sunshine in my life. I seem to bask in the most glowing memories of him; and not in memories only, but in the knowledge that we are with each other all the time.

I think of our wonderful intercourse, and again I read the letter of to-day:

"My dearest,

Yesterday we had lots of excitement. It didn't happen to me, though—my two patrols were quite uneventful, except that I was once just on the point of strafing an observation balloon, when I discovered that it was one of ours!

The excitement was over the exploit of two others—one of them a fellow who was in the tender that night when Hyatt left.

A Hun two-seater was met just over the lines at 17,000 feet. The pilot was heading east and our two were going west, so they attacked him and forced him down. His machine was faster than ours, but by manoeuvring they always kept to the east of him and made him lose height gradually.

The fight went on for forty-five minutes, and finally ended on the ground ten miles this side of our lines.

The Hun landed, and our people landed with him. A brand new machine, undamaged, and pilot and observer!

We collected the machine and it arrived on our aerodrome just before dinner.

Bv coincidence the C.O. had invited the Marine Light Infantry Band to give a concert in the Squadron, and so we had them playing in the mess during dinner. It made a celebration.

To-day is rather unpleasant. We left the old aerodrome for another nearer the line and everything is upset and uncomfortable at present.

We had breakfast at 6 a.m., and had to have everything packed by 7 a.m. Then the pilots flew their machines here and had to wait in cheerless wooden huts until the lorries with kit and furniture arrived.

Another fellow and I, however, cleared away early and explored the new district; finally coming to anchor in a very pleasant café-restaurant, where we had omelette, bread and cheese, red wine and coffee. When we got back here and found no lunch going we felt we had scored.

The weather is too bad for patrols; the clouds are thick and low.

I am looking at your photograph as I write. I love it. I love you. Darling, you matter so very much to me and I am so glad. Dear, dear Aimée.

I found myself wishing you were having that quaint lunch with me this morning. You would have thought it quite thrilling. That is what we will do often. Isn't it?

All my love to you, my wife,

BILL."

The tenderest wind rustles the trees and sways the daffodil stems. I don't feel it, yet the air is buoyant.

Between here and the rising slope a man, clad in earth-coloured clothes, is sowing a field. I see the even, semi-circular movement of his arm and the shower as it falls. He tramps steadily, there and back and there again once more.

I wonder what the sunshine means to him.

XI

WHAT do you think we are doing this morning? Why—sitting on the sea shore, staring out to sea!

Where the ripples break they make white surf—"wild white horses" tamed by the sun.

I have taken off my dress and shoes and stockings. What remains is a pair of wedge-wood blue "pantaloons," a blue jersey, and an enormous battered straw hat with a blue ribbon swathed round the crown to hold it together.

Molly wants to take a photograph to send to Bill.

I would love to have him here at this moment, but instead there is his letter, which the postman brought just as we started away in Polly Blue. I have kept it until now to read.

Down there Garry is up to his knees in water. He is like a white spot in the big ocean. Near him Nanny, holding her skirts high with one hand, and unconscious of the tail of soaked petticoat at the back, is searching the shingle— for something that may be turned into food or medicine or healing balm, I'm certain.

Further along the bank Molly is scribbling. The sky is blue. It is a perfect day.

I read:—

"My darling,

I had a most lovely letter from you yesterday.

Last night I read it again and thrilled with joy. My heart said he had something most important to say to you, but he would not tell me what. He insisted that he preferred to deliver the message himself and, though he didn't like waiting, he said it was more than worth it.

'It's a Wise Heart' I answered 'that knows his own love!'

I'm frightfully interested to hear of your idea for work.

With regard to what you speak of,

don't you think the material might be used to make 'Ad Astra' more complete?

Yesterday afternoon I did two patrols. One was for balloon strafing, but the balloons would not wait to be strafed. On the second one, however, Hyatt lost the patrol, was attacked by Huns, shot one down and got away.

To-day is dud—for the lines at least. I was up this morning for a joy ride and to practise 'stunting'. This after-noon Hyatt and I are going to ride into L—— to get a bath.

A new flight commander has just arrived. He was my instructor at home. Two of the present flight commanders are about due to go home for three months' rest, as they have been out nine months.

I've only eight months and a bit longer to go. Hooray!

We are not staying at this aerodrome for long; but when we move again it should be final.

I knew you'd hate the slip-shod flip-pancy of 'The Pretender.' I didn't read critically, but was just ready to be pleased with the 'Quartier' bits.

I think I understand perfectly and appreciate what you say about my being 'free.' But I find that I am not free—

not while I love you. Oh, darling, it is
the most enchanting bondage; the most
perfect happiness to feel that I am not
free because I love you so utterly. I adore
you.

BILL."

That being so the day is more perfect; the sun
god more passionate!... I thank him for my
lover and his love.

Now where do you think we have been? Why
in the sea, of course.

I wanted to swim out to where I imagined the
coast of France must lie, for then I should have
been nearer to you. I could have told you with
my lips all that I must write so impatiently; but
there again human limitation imposed its
fetters. I couldn't even know the satisfaction of
wondering beyond my depth. Alas, I swallow
the ocean at every stroke.

The shore is deserted. Tamarisk trees make a
screen from the fields, and from Polly Blue
who brought us here before the morning was
wake.

Through several villages she ran, then down
a long long country lane, ending suddenly right
on to the sea. The others had been before, but to
me it was a revelation.

Wouldn't all the small children from all the
big towns just revel in this place!

Almost I could be futile and persuade myself that it is callous to enjoy such tranquillity while others live in the turmoil of war. Yet sanely I know that my spell of leisure hurts no one, and adds greatly to my Bill's ease of mind.

I recall the munition factory with its ceaseless activity. With horror again realise the mechanism and inhumanity of industrial life; for many there are unacquainted with leisure—and by leisure may be counted only the time when one is alert in mind and body and has no task that must be done.

But war is not responsible.

The toilers must toil in any event. Work without contrast is an abomination!

But that's ancient history, isn't it?

Nanny has builded a fire—of stones and tin cans and sticks—against a bank. On it the kettle whistles—literally, for there's an invention in its make up to enable it to call attention to its state. Our rations are spread—pheasants' eggs taken from their preserving jars, war-bread, and Nanny's best friend, a teapot full of tea. Garry is to drink creamy milk instead, but of solid food he will stow away in his small interior as much as any of us, and at the same time he will gaze upon the ocean and seem to ponder with complete detachment. So, I suppose, are Admirals reared!

XII

FROM the garden I hear the mingled voices of the lawn mower and Molly and her family of one—and less obviously the song of the birds and the whisper of the trees.

The chintz curtains, drawn away on either side of the widely opened window, frame a picture at which I never weary of gazing.

Inside, too, there is nothing that does not please. It is so chaste.

Imagine plain cream walls and a darkly polished floor; and against these a single bed, of Jacobean design, and of dark wood, spread with a coverlet of blue-green chintz.

Imagine then an easy chair, a small book-case, and a table on which may remain, undisturbed, a medley of writing materials, letters, books, and cigarettes.

A narrow full-length mirror reflects a part of the scheme. Two candle-sticks complete it, except for a photograph of my Bill who—though he may seem just like other men to the uninitiated,—to me has the most beautiful face in the whole world.

His letter brings the contrast of excitement to this perfect calm. The first sentence, though, adds a touch of domesticity:—

"My darling,

You will be glad to hear that yesterday I succeeded in getting a very hot bath. It was at a hospital, for aged men and women, run by nuns.

This morning the weather is good for flying, and I did an O.P. at 8 a.m.

There was another big push on, and I was able to look down at it, but couldn't see much beyond the constant explosions of our artillery barrage, and in a few places the bits of trenches where our men were making a new line after this successful advance.

You will have missed a letter from me on the 29th. We were moving again and had a very uncomfortable day.

At 6.30 a.m. I was out on an O.P. with another fellow. I was leading, and after we had been over the lines half an hour, getting 'Archied' very badly, we lost each other in the mist, which was very thick.

There were no Huns about, so at the end of an hour I started to return to the new aerodrome and, through carelessness, took the wrong direction and went south.

After twenty minutes I failed to recognise the country and turned north on chance, struck an aerodrome, and found I was nearly forty miles away from here.

The fellow who went out with me is posted as 'missing.' He must have had engine trouble or lost his way and been taken prisoner.

During the morning two Huns came over our aerodrome at an enormous height and I was sent up to chase them.

It was quite absurd, as they had only to put their noses down and glide home while I was climbing up. When I got to 19,000 feet, they were no longer in the sky.

The day before yesterday I had a quaint experience in firing on the range.

As I told you before, we put out a target sheet, 6 ft. square, on the ground, and then go up and dive on it, firing short bursts with the Lewis gun.

It is rather trying, because you get so keen to sight properly on to the target, when you are coming down almost vertically, that you forget the ground is coming near.

Anyhow I dived six times altogether and emptied one dram of ammunition— 97 rounds (bullets).

Then I asked on coming down if I had hit the target at all.

'Oh, yes!' the gun-room man said quite eagerly; 'there's one shot on the target.'

'One hit out of ninety-seven shots,' I gasped.

'Yes, sir,' he replied, 'but you're the first to hit the target at all. It's been out five days too.'

I feel I would like to write down to the bottom of the page, just saying: 'I love you, Aimée,' many, many times. But if I did it would not convey my love for you.

I am thrilled anew every time I look at your face. My darling, I adore you.

All yours,

BILL."

By the same post came another letter.

"Bien, bien—Aimée,

Since writing to you before lunch a letter from you has arrived.

I read it and then came to my hut to look at your face again, and so now I will talk to you a little more.

The weather is very hot, and I am sitting in a deck chair outside my door.

A few moments ago an old thought struck me afresh and much more strongly.

I thought, suddenly, as I looked round

our little camp, of in how many camps I had sat just like that—writing and smoking—during the last three years.

First there was the Northern Cavalry Depôt, where I felt a foreigner in England, besides a stranger to soldiering; then there were the moors in Yorkshire, where I was pleased enough with my surroundings but impatient to see the war; then not long afterwards, sitting in the sweltering Gallipoli heat on a high ridge north of Suvla Bay, depressed and disgusted, I longed for France and the 'civilization' of the Western front.

Another five months and I was squatting on the muddy floor of a tiny dug-out north of Ypres, with my knees up to the level of my chin and my spirits higher than that; then again, as the summer came round, outside in the sun once more, but this time on a Bairnsfather farm just behind the Belgian frontier.

There were the aerodromes in England, and now finally here I am, an airman on active service. Ahead of me I see a neat row of shining silvered machines—and the third from this end is mine, my fighting scout.

Last night I learned the greatest cure for war pessimism.

It is to dine with an R.F.C. Mess in France.

The General commanding our Brigade and a Colonel from the Brigade were dining with us. Combine the ages of our C.O. (a major) and that of our two guests and the average is about 26 years.

And hear them talk and laugh. They do it, roughly in equal parts. Of course it is almost entirely shop talk, but it is the comical and quaint side of 'shop.'

I looked on as an impartial spectator. The picture was one of youth not sobered, but stimulated, by responsibility: graced, not by a heroic air, but by one of serenity; endowed with unfailing optimism and avowing but one object of hate—not the Hun but the perpetrator, whoever he may happen to be, of 'hot air.'

Nearly thirty people under twenty-five years old doing a vital part of the work on which a whole army may depend!

The lesson of optimism hit one most fully when one realized that this was but a tiny part of the great mobilization of youth.

I'm getting horribly heavy, darling. The only way to retrieve this letter is to tell you I love you. But I was going to do that anyway and I was dying to get to it.

I love you,

BILL."

XIII

A MOMENT ago the postman with the ginger beard that sticks out at right angles from his chin, stopped his absurd donkey at the gate and clambered down from the queerest, most imbecile cart. It is so miniature, seeming to have a spring inside for a seat. The old man looks like a "Jack-in-the-box" when the lid has been opened suddenly.

But between them they bring my letters from over the sea.

Was there ever, since the beginning, so beautiful a postman or donkey or cart?

I read:

"My wife,
I wrote last night describing a great and successful exploit of the Squadron yesterday morning. But on consideration I found that it would be unwise to send it through the post.

When the wheeze is no longer new I will describe it.

It was an experiment in balloon

strafing and it came off. Six of us attacked six balloons and we destroyed five. One fellow failed because his gun jammed like mine did that day, you remember?

I had eleven bullet holes in my machine and some of the others were nearly as bad.

This morning we got up against the whole Hun flying corps again.

We crossed the lines at 12,000 and saw two quirks trying to crawl away from a large formation of Hun Scouts—all red ones. We cut in between and stood over the Huns, who turned east again. We counted nine. They went out of sight, climbing, and re-appeared to the south obviously trying to get between us and the sun. We defeated them in that and outclimbed them too and then went straight at them—three of us.

They promptly turned east again and we never got within range. They are faster than us on the level.

This business went on for nearly an hour. The nine red Huns came back four times, heading for us very bravely, but every time we got into the sun and then went for them. They never stayed, and ultimately went away for good.

There was no mail yesterday and therefore I expect two letters from you to-day.

Later.

They have come—two lovely letters!

When you tell me how happy you are, darling, I am thrilled every time. My heart, as yours, is full of joy. All the time I have a glow of content I never knew before.

A few sentences in a letter from home increased my happiness. I think they will increase yours. Joan says 'Aimée seems to like to have mother's letters. Sometimes, when I come to think of it, if seems strange how much she is one of us. I think we all love her more the more we know her.'

Writing since to Joan I said how I value her words and asked:

'Wasn't our instinct right?'

Was it, bien-Aimée?

Yes, I really love the photograph. I look at it many times a day, and when I look I think of many wonderful and delicious things, and I tell it how I love you.

All yours, dearest one,

BILL."

XIV

DOWN in the Valley the tiny dull red village seems to be asleep.

Except for the ploughmen who harrow the patchwork fields there is no sign of life—and none of war.

Yet from every cottage almost a husband or sons have gone to the fight—sailors mostly, for the road, when it branches off, leads directly to our most special Navy port.

I think the Vale is like the calm face of a woman who hides in her breast the woe anxiety breeds.

I will read my letter again. I feel rather alone up here.

"My dearest one,

We are having things a good deal easier just now for some unknown reason. I really think that the period during which the Huns very seriously were threatening to be top dog in the air is at an end.

But the weather has been unspeakably fine since we changed our quarters, and we are all praying for a 'dud' day, so that we may feel free from flying for twenty-four hours.

I have just recalled something the Odd Man was telling us. He was saying how much his wife was learning of flying corps slang, and instanced her letter of the previous day, in which she said that the nurse was ill in bed, but added, 'However, the devil has had a 'dud' day with the children'!

Hurrah!... It has started to peal with thunder, and we are all delighted, I especially, for I can go on talking to you.

Nothing very thrilling has happened. I did a patrol last evening and another this morning, and saw no Huns on the first, but to-day there were quite a number about. I was up alone and saw two formations—one of three and another of four. I out-climbed them and headed for them, but they went away east.

．　　．　　．　　．

Ball's latest exploit is delicious.

About ten days ago, when the clouds were down at 2,000 feet, he went and 'sat over' the Hun aerodrome. Five Hun machines came up to strafe him, and he shot three down and made the other two crash on their own aerodrome.

The Odd Man has asked me to write an article for his magazine!

Really, I could do quite an interesting one on 'The Vicar as his parishioners do *not* know him.'

He is a wonderful person; a raconteur, a sportsman and a tomboy. Just now he is working hard trying to level the ground in the middle of our huts to make a tennis court.

On Sunday night I went to a service. There were about thirty of us in the ante-room of the —th Squadron Mess. The walls were thickly decorated with Kirchner and Pinot studies—of what I call the sublimely sacred—and cards were strewn on the tables. Before the service could start we had to cut off George Robey—in the middle of a doubtful song—on the gramophone.

The Odd Man explained that he wanted to make it a meeting rather than a service; therefore after prayers and a few hymns he proposed we should smoke while he gave us an address.

It stimulated thought, he said.

.   .   .   .

It is worth a good deal to see him on the aerodrome when any big stunt is going forward.

He was down there to watch us start for the balloon strafe. He was fearfully grave and just walked round the machines—hardly saying a word. I don't think he expected any of us to return.

I was the second to get back. The first was the one whose gun had jammed. I lost my engine on landing and stopped on the far side. The Odd Man sprinted out, beating the 'acc-emmas' (mechanics) by yards.

'Any luck?' he shouted. He was fearfully excited.

'Yes, it's all right,' I said.

'Oh, damn good!' he exclaimed. 'Damn good .... Absolutely topping!'

The others came in at intervals, and he beat the C.O. and everyone in welcoming them. He ran about from pilot to pilot, saying 'Damn good! ... How completely splendid!'

The C.O. joined him in a duet of jubilation and supplemented his 'damn good' by extracts from the new vocabulary.

.   .   .   .

I have just had instructions to go by tender to ——— to fly back a new machine. So I will finish this and post it without waiting to see if there is a letter from you.

All my most passionate love,

BILL."

XV

THERE are times when I long, beyond reasoning, for a sight of my beloved—to hear his voice, too; to touch his mouth, to lie with his arms wound about my body, and to breathe his breath. It was so last night, and I wept. To-day I am a philosopher again. My letter brings me nothing but joy:—

"My darling wife,

I got your letter before lunch. It thrilled me more than any. I want you, I love you intensely—oh, so much! I dare not think of our next meeting. It is too—too wonderful to contemplate!

.   .   .   .

The trip to X—— to fetch the new machine did not turn out as I expected, but very much better.

When I arrived at the sheds there and was almost ready to start, the C.O. turned up, with the Odd Man, in his own car and said he would fly back, as he wished to get home immediately. We could return together he said.

So we watched him start away. In the

meantime the weather had picked up and was gorgeous, so I had a good idea that there would be work going about.

But the Odd Man said that was all right. He had seen to it for me and we could stay and have dinner at X——.

First we had tea at the Pool, where one meets everyone one ever knew in the Flying Corps—and then motored into the town with much dignity; I with my stream-line fittings and the Odd Man with his dark blue, and light blue and red brassard on his sleeve bearing the letters R.F.C.

We drew up at the big French café in the square, and there 'degusted' each two *Dubonnets*; and then went to the Restaurant V—— for a perfect little dinner.

Having been happy in our choice of a white wine we allowed it to circulate well and came out to the big green car behind our cigars, feeling that for one night at least nothing could interrupt our tranquility.

.   .   .   .

This morning we—the C.O. and your husband—left the aerodrome at 4.45 in semi-darkness. It was an early bird effort to catch the Hun worm, but the sky was empty, so about a mile over the German side of the trenches the C.O., who is a stunt pilot, did a few turns.

He started by a loop. I promptly followed. He 'chucked' two more and so did I. Then he did a series of 'Immelmann turns' so quickly that, watching him from the ground, you would have sworn he was flying upside down most of the time.

A few hundred yards away I was hard at the same thing.

The Huns down below must have wondered.

I wound up the show by two of my best spins of 1,000 feet each.

.   .   .   .

The Odd Man has finished the tennis court and we have started a tournament. I am down with him, and while he is easily one of the best players I am easily the worst. I have been sent for, so—Au Revoir, ma bien-Aimée. I love you.

BILL.

P.S.—I forgot to say that the cheques you have written will be all right.

As for it being a strain—why I am intensely happy and amazingly content.

It is first because of our love and then because I know you, too, are happy and contented in your surroundings.

A strain! My darling, even if it *were*— but it is a delight. It is wonderful to feel that I am making someone happy because I was afraid I might never be able to do that. It is lovely to know I can—and yet it is so little I do.

BILL."

I, also, find it wonderful to be able to make someone happy.

I think most of us have it in our power to do so only if we are met half way, and I can make Bill glad because he wants me to, and because he gives all of himself in response.

One feels so powerful—and yet so humble, too.

XVI

TO-DAY we passed along a roadway cut through a wood and then, at the other end, came upon a village apparently composed of a few cottages, several houses standing in acres of ground, and a church.

It was the most fascinating church I have ever seen. The inside was white-washed and the oak beams were black and uneven with age. There was brass exquisitely designed, and lilac and wild apple-blossom stood upon the altar.

A list of vicars from the 14th century hung outside the studded door.

Leading to it, of course, were the inevitable tombstones, some so ancient that the moss completely covered them.

One grave was quite new.

I hated to think of the decaying body under the earth.

Two old men hobbled past us as we re-started Polly Blue. They were all we saw of human life.

"How do they manage to live so long?" I asked of Molly, as though she should know.

"Why not?... There's nothing to make them die here, is there?" she said.

We heard the boom of a gun practising at the naval port across the hills.

Nothing to make them die,—and so much death not far away!

Soon we returned to our glorious circle of the Downs. Our village is like a plainer woman with a subtle imagination—much more enticing companion!

A letter from Bill had arrived by the afternoon post. I ran up here, to my own den, to read:—

"My sweet wife,
Nearly a month has gone already!

Yesterday was Sunday and a day of 'hate' as usual.

I was on the mid-day patrol with my flight commander, Captain Romney, and about half way through we spotted two Hun scouts a good way over the other side. We climbed round them and dived.

Romney, who goes in for getting right up to his Hun before firing, approached to within 40 yards of the first one and then fired ten rounds.

The Hun did an Immelmann turn and came out on Romney's tail. Romney did the same, got off another burst and the Hun dived away. I saw only the first manoeuvre, for I was diving on the second one. But mine didn't wait to do any Immelmann turns. I started firing at about 100 yards, and put 30 rounds into him. The Hun went on diving, and so fast that I could not gain any more.

The Artillery people on the ground reported one of the Huns crashed! They had watched the fight. We don't know whose it was but think mine.

In the afternoon Romney got one again. There were four of us out, but he got so close to the Hun—a two-seater—and sat so persistently under his tail that we could not get near and dare not fire.

Ultimately the Hun went down burning, and that was confirmed from the ground.

.　　.　　.　　.

This morning when we returned from early morning patrol there was a new balloon strafe on the tapis.

I was sitting opposite the C.O. at breakfast—imagine a tousle-headed youth in pyjamas and a flying coat, for he had been called up early to organise the raid—and he asked me if I would go again. I said 'yes.'

Romney, however, intervened, and said he was entirely against anyone doing it twice. He proposed, however, that the remainder of the squadron should be sent up to 'demonstrate' over the balloons and distract attention from the 'contour chasers.'

.　　.　　.　　.

I was late in getting off the aerodrome and the raiders had got over the lines before I was in a position to see them. I had to climb, you see.

However from miles away I watched three balloons start burning and collapse.

Tootling round I spotted three more balloons a good deal south of the ones we had to attack, and went over to investigate.

Three machines were flying behind them—Hun two-seaters.

I spiralled down above them to have a nearer view and when at about 1,200 yards' range, I heard one of them firing. So I changed my spiral into a dive on to the nearest one and heard the gun going again. Then they dived too and eastward. Next moment I knew the reason, for five of our new scouts came tearing past taking up the chase.

Soon the whole eight were out of sight.

I turned round, and being now only a couple of thousand feet above the balloons I thought I'd have a go at one.

I didn't get far. They had been watching me too long from the ground and immediately I was greeted with machine guns. The tracer bullets came up in silver streaks and the next minute there was a nasty cough behind as their anti-aircraft fired its ranging shot.

I didn't wait, but tootled home.

The second raid was quite a success. Six balloons were destroyed, but one of our fellows is missing.

.   .   .   .

Last night we had an officer from the Army Headquarters to mess. He came to tell us how bucked the infantry people were with what our squadron had done in the first balloon strafe.

I hear that the post is just going out. I loved your letter this morning.

I love you.

BILL."

XVII

LAST night propped up against my pillows reading Bill's thrilling experiences over again, I came to this, which at breakfast time seemed quite unimportant.

"Two letters have come from Greta de Jeunaisse.

"You remember—I told you how kind she and her mother were to me in Paris?... She writes from there telling me all the latest news, and she finishes:—

"'Your greeting, and above all your portrait, have given me great delight.... You do not tell me when you are coming to Paris. I am impatient to see you once more.'"

It was midnight—a time when things come to us poignantly—and I began to wonder if this

Greta holds the very French notion that Bill's marriage is one of convenience and that—having written and sent his photograph in answer to the letters which followed him about and reached him only after his marriage—he is eager for an "affaire."

Although I want him to feel free as the wind, I couldn't help writing to point out that Latin women have the foresight not to believe in so-called Platonic friendship. As a matter of fact I scarcely can imagine even an Englishwoman expressing her impatience to see again the man who had told her of his wife. In theory it sounds ridiculous, but practically it is impossible for any man—unless he wishes to be taken seriously—to show appreciation of any feminine human being who is not old enough to be his mother or young enough to be his child.

It is true—and the reverse is true also. Almost any woman could, with the opportunity, make any man who is not blindly loving some other woman, think lovingly of her.

To-day's letter is so thrilling that my thoughts seem trivial.

"Dearest one,

I got a Hun yesterday afternoon. It was a great scrap and I was fearfully pleased, because for the first time in a scrap I tried a pukka Immelmann turn and brought it off. I was with Romney and when we were at 16,500, about five miles over the lines, he dived on two Hun two-seaters at about 14,000.

I saw him go down and pass right underneath and then I went for the other.

It was a big bus with polished yellow wooden body and green wings. At about 100 yards I started firing, and the Hun, who was going across me, turned and climbed round as if to get on my tail.

Then came my Immelmann! With engine full on, I pulled the machine up hard and nearly vertical. When she was almost stalling I kicked her left hand rudder hard and the machine whipped over on one wing, turned her nose down, and came out exactly in the opposite direction.

The Hun was now dead in front of my gun about 200 feet below me. I opened on him again and almost immediately he started diving and slowly spinning.

To keep my gun on him I had to go down absolutely vertical, and eventually went beyond the vertical and found myself on my back with the engine stopped through choking.

When at length I fell into a normal attitude again, the Hun had disappeared. One of our patrols which had come over in time to see the scrap says he went down spinning and crashed.

.   .   .   .

This morning I was detailed to lead a patrol—my first.

It might have been a success but for 'Archie.'

I headed over the lines and crossed at 10,000 feet. Then war broke out and for several minutes I couldn't see the two fellows who were following, for the black shell bursts all around us.

To put the A-A gunners off their range I side-slipped and stunted and then climbed above a cloud. The others did the same.

It was only a small cloud, however, and soon came to an end. Promptly on reappearing we got another salvo and I felt a violent shock on the 'joy-stick.' The whole machine shuddered, but before I had begun to wonder what had been hit I stuck my nose down hard and due west. Everything looked all right.

Leaning out and peering round the engine cowling I found the under carriage still there. I waggled the 'joy-stick.' The tail controls were all right. Again I waggled the 'joy-stick.' Wing controls all right. But no, nothing happened. I looked at the ailerons. The left one moved, but the right one did not move.

Then I glanced at the aileron controls. Just against my screen the right aileron control had been shot away!

I kept my nose down, heading for home, and found that I could still get a sufficient amount of wing controls to make slow turns. Landing became a problem, as the moment I switched off the engine the right wing dropped. I flew right on to the ground, though, without smashing anything.

I have the broken parts of the rod and the armourer is going to produce some souvenir from it for you.

. . . .

I have read and read again your last few letters. They made me so wonderfully happy, longing for you ever so impatiently, yet curiously content to wait; just loving you, darling, with all the passion I own.

All yours,

BILL."

After reading that I wonder if it would be dreadfully foolish of me to post my misgivings about Greta.

Somehow I feel I want him to share all that

passes through my mind. He deserves the truth.

Some men would dismiss this, thinking it to be the sort of jealousy by which married people are supposed to make life a burden to one another.

There *is* a tinge of jealousy of course—but it is something deeper which makes me want to speak. I can't express what I think. It is very difficult.

XVIII

"ALL my own darling.

I am in the orderly room relieving the orderly officer for dinner, and I want to talk to you.

Every day I am more staggered by this amazing life. It is the contrasts in it, the abrupt changes that make it so astounding.

Before lunch I was sitting in a cosy mess writing to my wife. At tea-time I was fifteen miles over the lines, flying over Hun land, aiming my gun, and shooting to kill. And then, later, changed into clean clothes, I dined in comfort, unsurpassed even in England just now.

Yesterday we went over to another

squadron, where the C.O. was to fly a Hun machine—an Albatross Scout—against one of ours. The idea was to test them for speed level, climbing, diving, and turning, and then to have a scrap. We expected some good flying, but the whole was a wash-out as the engine went dud.

It is to be tried again to-morrow, and I am to fly one of our machines against the C.O.

Captain Kyrle crashed this morning in the trenches. His engine stopped and he turned upside down about 500 yards behind the front line. A big artillery strafe was going on at the time, and he couldn't get out of the machine, but just had to hang there head first, by his belt, listening to the big shells crumpling all around.

At last some Canadians managed to run out and release him from the wreckage. They took him into their dug-out, and when things got quieter he came away.

There's a hell of a lot of strafing every day, and the sky in the east is vivid all night through.

The weather refuses to break, and it is oppressively hot. You would love it, I know. But we are longing for a real break. We want a rest from patrols for a day or two.

I quite forgot to tell you about Hyatt. He had claimed three Huns, and a fortnight ago was put on a roving commission—that is to say he was left to fly when he liked and where he liked, provided he got Huns.

One day he went up late and came back at dusk. He said he had been a long way over the lines and had met three Huns. Two he shot down on their own aerodrome and the third dived away.

Going along further south he picked up a single machine and later saw five Huns. Thinking he had the assistance of the scout he had picked up he dived at the five. Hardly had he started than the scout fired at him from behind. He turned round and climbed and discovered black crosses on the scout.

It was a Hun!

Getting under this Hun he put his gun up, emptied his drum, and saw the Hun dive down and into a pond!

Then Hyatt came home.

Two days later—that is three days ago—he crashed on landing. He was not damaged but said he had hurt his head. He is now at the hospital here and says he can't remember anything.

He had to be informed that there is a

war on and that the French are fighting with us. He recalls London vaguely. Fortunately he recognises his wife's photograph.

So Hyatt may be home with her shortly.

Later.

The post has come bringing the lovely letter you wrote in bed.

Your doubt about Greta's attitude brought doubt to me for the first time. In any event there will be no chance of my going to Paris at present.

Tuesday Evening.

The post is going now. I send you all my love.

My wife!

BILL."

XIX

I HAVE climbed to the highest point of the Downs to let the wind blow through and round me.

So many thoughts have tangled themselves in my brain and now that they are weeded out I want to tell of them.

It all started, of course, with Bill's remark: "In any event there will be no chance of my going to Paris at present."

"That means," I said to myself, "that *were* there a chance he would go without me!.... Why then, did I not go to Italy with Desirée instead of refusing because I knew he wanted us to go together afterwards.... And he would see his Greta!... Why then have I made a resolve not even to write to any of those men who easily might persuade themselves that he—although my husband—is not my dearest love?"

Then I was aghast.

"What," I exclaimed. "Have I descended to this?"

My dear and I have discovered that we are able to accompany one another into our most intimate thought gardens; and I know he will understand that, afterwards, I tried to pull the weeds—that's all.

So I reasoned.

"Bill's and my marriage has in it the possibilities of perfect Romance. He is most beloved of me; yet if, now or at any time, he lightly should appreciate our Romance—and with so fragile a flower to be careless and to kill were the same—then which should I regret. Him or Romance?"

Why Romance, of course; for there are other

men and other interests, but seldom the possibility of pure Romance!

Now the garden is clear once more.

I love him—this dear, dear lover of mine.

XX

"MY darling Aimée,

After writing you yesterday I found that I was due out on the next patrol.

It was the most uncomfortable patrol I have ever had. Romney led and a new pilot—an excellent one—made the third.

We climbed all out and when a good way over saw a Hun two-seater. Romney gave chase and it headed north-east.

I don't know for how long we followed, but we gained slowly, and at last Romney dived.

As he did so the Hun fired three rockets, evidently a signal.

Romney fired at close range and sheered off. The Hun observer fired back at him as the pilot dived. I then went down vertically after him firing dead on and did not stop until my drum was empty. The

Hun was still going down—falling. He had not fired at me and we believe both pilot and observer had been hit.

I started climbing while changing my empty drum for a full one, and, looking around, saw two scout machines above me.

'Romney and Grahaeme' I thought; and proceeded leisurely, climbing up to them.

One of the pilots put his nose down and came towards me, and next moment I heard the familiar and horrid 'Pop-pop-pop.'

They were firing at me. It certainly was neither Romney nor Grahaeme.

As I had feared all through the chase the Hun two-seater had been a lure and now I was in a trap. They had a thousand feet of height on me, so I put my nose westward and downward, and, glancing round, saw they were doing the same.

By losing height steadily I was able to keep up speed, but I hadn't realised how far east we had come. It seemed hours before I saw the trenches in the distance—actually it was fifteen minutes before I reached them.

All the time the Huns were firing short bursts, but I was never going straight for three seconds together. I kicked the rudder and slid flat from one side to another, and at last as I crossed the reserve Hun trenches—now at less than 3,000 feet—I saw the Hun machines turn away.

It wasn't all over though, for, first, tracer bullets came up from the ground and, after I had dived and side-slipped to avoid them, the anti-aircraft guns put up a barrage in front of me. For five minutes I turned and twisted to throw them off and finally got over our trenches at 1,000 feet.

Later I heard that when Romney had stood off after he too had been attacked by two Hun scouts, but being on their level he had climbed away from them. One of his planes had been badly ripped by the fire from the first Hun we attacked.

The third fellow had seen us diving and looking around saw four Hun scouts coming out of the clouds. He went to have a look at them and then got lost in the clouds. It was half an hour before he found his way back to the lines.

.   .   .   .

I haven't told you about the Air Hog! He is an excellent fellow really, but he takes things frightfully seriously and is simply crazy to get Huns. His air-hoggishness was revealed early—when he came into the mess announcing that he was going on a 'jolly old patrol.'

It was the first time we had ever heard it so called. Most of us use something much more sanguinary.

However, he went out a few times and then developed a habit of going up and tearing about the sky all alone.

He went Hun-strafing mad. If he saw a Hun five miles away and chased it for ten minutes he hardly would be able to contain himself, and would talk about what a 'jolly old patrol' it had been.

At last he was put on the roving commission game and since then has spent eight hours a day at least in the air.

When it is not fit for patrol he mopes and frets, and worries everybody about the weather; and doesn't improve because he fails to get any sympathy from us.

Later.

Two letters from you, glowing about your work—the revision of the play and the articles—and smelling of your lovely perfume.

It is brilliantly fine again. I'll be flipping soon.

Dear, dear wife, I love you.

BILL."

Bill, couldn't you just manage to "flip" over the edge of the Downs? You are so near, really. If you were to go up into the sky with the wind behind, you could be here with me, in this room, in one little hour. Think what it would mean to me. And I'd let you go back again after I had covered you with kisses and listened to your voice, telling me of your love!

XXI

"BIEN Aimée,

The Squadron did a thrilling exploit last night. It went bathing at midnight. The Odd Man, of course, was the leader.

Some miles away there is a most topping valley occupied by a chateau and its grounds. A river runs through it and about a week ago the C.O. and the Odd Man got permission from the people at the chateau to dam the stream—or, as the Odd Man prefers to put it, 'to erect an artificial barrier across the stream—in order to form a swimming pool.'

The Squadron did the work and it was finished yesterday. After dinner the C.O.

suggested that we should all go and bathe in the pool.

We had a tender and fifteen of us went—some of us armed with pocket lamps and all attired in pyjamas, towels and flying coats.

The water was beautifully deep and clean; and it was eerie to see the naked bodies scrambling about the barrier of tree trunks amongst the shadows thrown by the huge monsters on the bank.

The Odd Man was the noisiest of the crowd.

He did high dives into the black pool, shouting and splashing like a water baby.

To-day four of the fellows have developed colds, and even the Odd Man is a little off colour. I tell him that midnight revels with water nymphs do not suit him.

But I haven't told you of my expedition!

Yesterday, with the C.O.'s permission, I travelled for many hours on a motor-bicycle—seeing the war. I had tea with a General, and supper with a sergeant.

The sergeant was Dick. Supper consisted of bottled Bass and a cake from home.

It was a frantic business, finding where his brigade was. After touring the larger part of Northern France I entered Z——, and ran into a fellow I knew, who is now C.R.E.—that is to say officer in charge of works.

He took me along to H.Q., and there I found where the Division and the Brigade were. Then I went to the Town Commandant's billet with my pal and had tea with General ———, to whom I hot-aired about flying for half an hour.

At last I got out of the town and found Dick at the wagon lines. To get there I had to pass through a belt of most amazing country—the piece of ground that for two years until last month held our own trenches, the Hun trenches, and no man's land.

The sight cannot be described.

It is as if roads and villages and woods and fields suddenly had become liquid like a sea, and had rolled themselves over and over in huge waves—stopping abruptly at their most fantastic moment.

I found Dick in a little tin hut with his Sergt.-Major, Q.M.S., and the other sergeants—all good fellows.

He was looking wonderfully fit and was in excellent spirits.

I went to the officer's mess also and was awfully well received. They spoke glow-ingly and quite spontaneously of Dick.

Writing home I have told Mother that they have described him as a 'damned good lad with lots of guts!'

They told me about his Military Medal exploit. It was during the bombardment prior to the advance.

The Huns barraged the road on which the ammunition teams were working between the dump and the batteries, and smashed up several teams. Just when everything was horribly confused, Dick came along and, irrespective of who was who, and in the thick of the shelling, organised some order out of chaos and blood.

A few days ago he was congratulated personally by the Divisional G.O.C.

I gather that his C.O. is quite keen on Dick's prospects for a commission. And so am I. It has been good for him to start from the beginning, but now it is time for him to move on.

I got home at 10 a.m. It was a topping experience.

Most happily yours,

BILL."

XXII

COULD a woman know greater joy than this? Listen:

> "For whom I live.
>
> Your long letter of Monday night has come.
>
> I love your idea of Romance.... It is all mine. I will treasure and guard Romance, embodying you, so jealously. But you have made me realise how it may be destroyed by the merest want of thought and in spite of the most sincere loyalty.
>
> This letter thrills me more than any. I have read it many times.
>
> Darling Aimée, I love you! I love you! I am all yours. It makes me deliriously happy to know we are so much to each other that is satisfying and more than that.
>
> Since you mention it, I may as well refer again to my remark about going to Paris. You never could believe to yourself that I would choose to go on leave anywhere without you.
>
> Dear, I am living for you: I want you,—I can't tell you how I love you!

I have told you often that I am curiously content. But it is not complacency, and I know you know that. My contentment is made up of the most wonderful memories and the most wonderful promise—and of your and my own happy philosophy of life. Oh, bien-Aimée!

And yet I may go to Paris and alone! Until quite recently pilots used to be sent there for new machines, and maybe this will happen again. It is not likely, however, that I should go, and if I did I would not visit Greta.

In this case and in any case, I not only see your point but agree with you. I must admit I had not seen the danger of it as applying to myself, but already I had made up my mind neither to write to, nor to see her, for a long time.

Darling Aimée, I love you. I love you to the exclusion of everything in life but your happiness; and that is my happiness, too. I love you beyond all measure.

It is ecstacy to say 'My wife.'

And I am all yours.

BILL."

Bill, you are perfect. You make me your slave—no, more than that, your friend—when you understand like that!

XXIII

PURCELL has borrowed my favourite weapon to write the laundry list.

She came in and said:

"I'm sure, Miss, you must have collected all the pencils in the kitchen last night."

I don't know why she wants to write a laundry list on Whit-Sunday; but it never would do for me to say so. Certainly if I tried to prevent her she would go and 'munition,' and then this household would tumble to pieces altogether.

The window is opened wide; but outside there are no Downs, no trees, no distance—only a 'thin piece of sky' and dozens and dozens of chimney pots and the two top storeys of a building, loftier than the rest.

I can't see the street, for I am too high above it and too far back in the room; but the whirr of traffic is unavoidable. An instant ago there was a pause like the quiet at a table where everyone has been talking; but already a motor-lorry—the boisterous one of the party—flings itself into the vacancy.

This is town!

So much has happened that I can't recall why I decided—originally—to come here. Oh, yes, I do remember. Molly's parents wrote. They wished to visit her for a week if arrangements would allow for their entertainment.

Knowing that my room would be needed, I said "Au Revoir," to it regretfully, and looked up the best through train for London.

The garden, where the trees cast shadows under which we had sat to worship Nature in her loveliness, seemed more beautiful than ever because I should not see it again for many days.

Until the moment came to leave I followed Garry in and out along familiar paths that make a mysterious fairyland for him. I think it is cruel for children to live away from gardens. They should grow with the flowers and the grass. These and the birds should be their story books.

And now, having come to town, I seem to be involved in the most thrilling episodes.

Really they all, indirectly, are the outcome of a sisterly letter which arrived a week or two ago from Maisie:—

"Dear Amy," she wrote—and that's the sisterly touch in chief, for she refuses to recognise the picturesque translation of my name—"I've just read a thing of yours that I found lying about the house. I know you'll be wild, for you're such an ass about anyone seeing anything; but

anyway I don't see why you shouldn't
pull yourself together and be businesslike
and try to make some money for a change.
I'm sure you've cost mother enough one
way and another.

"I'm glad to say you write better than I
expected, though I think you ramble on a
bit too much. You should come to the
point quicker. We're in a hurry now-a-
days, and much too tired to wonder what
it's all about.

"Anyway don't trouble to alter what
you've done. I'll bring it up-to-date myself if necessary. I've given this thing to
a man who knows the editor of the
'Philanderer,' which is decidedly the
smartest magazine of the moment. Now
don't get in a temper about it. It's for your
own good.

"Love,

"MAISIE."

This letter had its use, besides supplying Molly
with amusement, for it provoked me to
despatch a bundle of MS to the agent upon
whose advice, she had heard, one could rely.

I suppose it's a form of self-consciousness,
or as Maisie would put it, "conceit," that makes
some of us avoid spectators. Until my marriage
I shrank from the idea that anyone who knew

me should read my thoughts; but having lived
with Bill, who is so much more open and gener-
ous in his outlook, I seem to mind less and less.

Then the day before leaving the country this
came:—

> "Dear Madam,
>   I have read the MS sent to me by your
> sister, and I find it quite good. It is too
> long, however, as we do not consider
> serials, but we would be glad if you would
> submit, before Thursday next, a short
> story of 800 words.
>   Yours truly,
>
>   ———."

I hadn't a short story of any length and I hadn't
the fogiest idea for one.

"I'll simply write and say so," I said to
Molly, who came as usual to my room after
breakfast to discuss the post.

"Good gracious, no," she cried. "You must
have a try at least."

Then I realised that, of course, I must have a
try and, what is more, a successful try.

Maisie's words also seemed like the truth—I
had "rambled on too long."

So all that day I sat at my table, and after
dinner exchanged the result for an article that
Molly had been doing—in her airy fashion—on

Rhodesia, which became less vague to me as I read.

And as she found my effort very much to her taste we afterwards went to bed rather hilariously.

Our gods chastened us soon enough for that. They sent Molly's article back to roost; and mine rendered their blow through the Editor of the "Philanderer," when several days later I sat in his office beside his desk.

"Yes; it's good enough in its way," he said. "But what our readers want is something more obvious than that!"

He had grey hair and a pince-nez and a keen clever face.

"Why does he prostitute his conception of things?" I wondered, saying aloud at the same time: "I'll do another then and let you have it to-morrow."

"Can you?" he asked.

"Of course," I answered, "if I choose."

What I should have said was: "Of course not, because I don't choose"—but to be baffled by the obvious pleased me little enough.

At home—the place where I used to house myself before my marriage to Bill—it seems impossible to work. The pandemonium of traffic rages night and day. Except to-day there is no privacy either, for now my old room has been commandeered.

"You can use mine if you don't expect me not to come in when I like; and you'll have to sleep on the inside, and not wriggle all the time!" Maisie said.

And as she spoke she arranged her head at the left-hand top corner and her feet at the right-hand lower corner of the bed. Until dawn and after that I tossed about open-eyed, disconnectedly piecing together the accursed short story.

"A man and a woman, and the other man or the other woman—that's the obvious," I thought; but what to make them do or say in the space of eight hundred words was as distant from me as sleep in the space left over by Maisie's adamant body.

When Purcell entered with the tea tray she awoke.

"You've kicked me all night in your sleep," she grumbled.... "I feel as though I'd been beaten black and blue!"

I looked at her—too wrath for speech.

"Well, don't let your eyes tumble out of your head," she growled, "and give me some tea for the love of glory.... I shall be ill if I have to share my bed again!"

Then the desperate inspiration came. The outcome of which was that the Babes—in whose opinion I have soared since presenting them with a brother-in-law—superintended a collection of food while I gathered together my pencil and writing pad and wits.

Joyously, before the dew had given itself to the sun, we spread our rugs under the biggest tree on the stretch of green overlooking the round pond.

I placed the Babes before me. "It doesn't matter what you do" ... I said ... "if you don't talk to me before it is time to eat."

"May we go out of sight then?" asked Bey.

"No, you may not ... and you mayn't fall into the water either," I replied.

So Betty arranged herself on her stomach, propped up by her elbows, and began to read a book; while Bey, strutting about, crooned nonsense to a one-eyed Teddy bear.

I think we had chocolate and buns and hard-boiled eggs for lunch and I know that by tea-time my tale was complete. Last evening the Editor man rang up to say he liked it very much; but suggesting an alteration to the last line, and that destroyed the redeeming touch of sincerity, adding spice, I admit, but spice of the most blatant sort—spice for the gourmand rather than for the gourmet.

"You don't mind?" he said.

"Not in the slightest," I replied—and neither did I, for I hadn't been baffled by the obvious after all.

. . . .

Just now Bill's letters have to be absorbed between events instead of being the one event of the four-and-twenty hours, but they are not less precious because of that.

They are my life. I have one for every day in the week. To-day there is no post, but two came yesterday—one by the first delivery and one by the last. Here is the earlier one:—

"My bien-Aimée,

For the first time this month a day without a letter from you. Because you were travelling, I suppose.

It is a perfect summer day and already I have done three hours flying, and later I am to lead a patrol!

I was out of bed this morning at 4 o'clock and in the air before it was properly light. It was quite an inoffensive patrol, for there were no Huns about— and it was a topping morning.

Breakfast was ready at 5.30, and after it I went to bed for two hours. Then at 10 a.m. I went out for a joy-ride. I flew up the line to Z—— and then tootled all round the salient and billets and bits of trench I had lived in last year.

On the way back I landed at another aerodrome and met half a dozen fellows who were at the home aerodrome with me.

You remember the second 'Hun'* whose argument with a hay-stack I described? He has had a further adventure.

While I was out on the aerodrome yesterday afternoon I heard Romney order my machine to be brought out. I hurried to ask if I was wanted for a patrol.

'No,' he said, 'I'm going to send up the hay-stack expert again.'

Fortunately my 'bus was not ready. Some alterations were being made to the cowling.

Another pilot had the misfortune to land at that moment and the 'Hun' was put into his machine. This time he got off the ground with a series of ungraceful hops, and once in the air did quite well.

Then he tried to land.

At the first essay he came in hundreds of feet too high and had the sense to open up the engine and fly round again.

The second time he came in much lower but still much too high. In spite of our shrieks and waving of caps and sticks he came down very fast right across the aerodrome, touched the ground about twenty yards from the further edge and

---

* "Hun" in this case means a beginner.

then ran between a hangar and some cottages; fell six feet into a sunken road and stood on his nose!

I don't forget I've been a 'Hun' myself, but . . . .

I've got a new stunt. Romney is enthusiastic about it.

It is called 'rolling.'

While the machine is going forward it is made to turn over sideways on to its back and to continue turning until it is normal again.

I told you the incident about B——, a great 'Hun-strafer,' who got up against some Boche stunt pilots and had to 'stop the fight' to watch them stunting.

This was the principal trick they were doing.

I hadn't the vaguest idea how it was done until some days ago when I was trying to improve on my 'Immelmann' turn. I hope if I ever meet a lot of Huns they'll stop the fight to watch me too.

Our hut looks lovely now—all draped a pale blue and with darker blue curtains and neat shelves and bookcases and pale blue bed-hangings.

But I want *you*, my wonderful lover. I long for you so much. Many times I do not sleep but think of you instead, and my thoughts are so thrilling. I love you, dearest woman.

All yours,

BILL."

I have been thinking that in all my experience I seldom have seen a woman and a man mated as Bill and I are mated.

At the best, in most cases, something has to be sacrificed for the sake of the something that is enjoyed.

There are those who are companionable mentally, but who draw one another by no charm. There are those who appeal emotionally and whose minds will be strangers until the end—and at the end more strange than now.

But when Bill calls me his "wonderful lover" I know it is because our minds, our senses, our spirits make, in communion, the harmony that is complete.

XXIV

THE short story was an incident merely, Molly's agent supplied the climax.

Feeling sick with the obvious I longed to take the nasty taste from my mouth and wondered how to do it. "I know," I thought suddenly, "I'll go to see the person 'upon whose advice one may rely'; and if he doesn't approve of what was sent to him Bill and I can become tinkers, or two-step experts, or we might contrive a risky acrobatic turn on the ceiling of a music hall. Anyway we needn't scribble any more."

The building was in one of those streets between the river and the Strand. As the lift-lady looked much too comfortable to be disturbed, indifferently I climbed the stair and, having knocked at a door, gave my name to a male thing so ponderously minute that I think he must have stepped from his cradle to take this serious part in life.

Then, as one of the many benefits acquired by my amazing marriage is a less feverish desire for the haste that accomplishes nothing, complacently I stood by a window watching a vividly green creeper grow up the side of the brick foundation to a row of chimney pots.

It was a miracle of nature where all else was artifice except the sky.

After some time the war-baby re-appeared to conduct me to another room where, immediately, I felt a most curious sensation of relief.

For here, whatever might ensue, was one who must detest the obvious as surely as Bill and I detest it.

.　　.　　.　　.

When a big thing happens in our lives I think we are more normal than when some trivial excitement occurs.

During the weeks preceding my marriage, I was serene; and since then the serenity has grown, yet happenings have been colossal.

And, in that room, listening to words which revealed a justification of our work together, I felt that it was not news to me—and yet it was!

It was news of the most beautiful sort for Vagabonds—promising freedom from the routine arranged by others; giving immunity from all purpose but our own.

There are those I know who uphold the slavery of system, and I myself agree that there are laws to be obeyed—but the machinery of life is for those who demand their problems cut and dried. It's neither for Bill nor for me nor for those who, like us, would explore.

Yet we must justify ourselves at least by evidence that we are willing to cope with the problem of every day.

We are too apt, I know, to sneer at the practical means of livelihood while still we eat and drink.

.   .   .   .

Calmly spoke the man "upon whose advice one may rely."

That very day, he said, proofs of articles accepted by the "Daily ——" had been returned from the censor: 'to be passed by the writer's C.O.' The same permission would be necessary for part of the material to form the book, for which there should be no difficulty in finding a publisher.

"And you know," he concluded, "with this paper crisis the sooner it is put in hand the better."

At first I thought I would telegraph to Bill, and then, realising nothing could be gained in that way, I wrote enclosing the proof, to be sent back immediately with the necessary sanction.

Now I wait—impatient that a few more days must elapse.

I feel that if I could be certain Bill had shared my joy I would be content.

Those who love should know no barrier of space nor distance.

It is very stupid.

> "My dearest One," he writes in the second letter.
>
> "Two perfectly lovely letters have come. They were sent last Saturday and Sunday from London.
>
> Darling, how every detail of what you do and think thrills me. I love you.
>
> I am sorry my first letter, addressed to town, was not in time, but you have it and more by now.

After writing to you yesterday I did a short patrol. The clouds were very low and apparently there was nothing doing—but later a call came through reporting a Hun machine 'spotting' for the artillery near ———. I was sent up to look for it.

I got into the clouds at 2,500 feet and did not clear them under 6,000. Then I went due east by compass and when I thought I was far enough over I dived through.

I came out at 2,000 feet dead over the trenches, so up I went into the clouds again and found myself about two miles further on. I patrolled for ten minutes just under the clouds and saw no Hun and came home above the clouds.

I led my patrol of five not too badly last night, I think, but 'Archie' dealt rudely with us and I simply couldn't—and the others couldn't—keep the formation.

We went a good way east and got 'Archied' there. I spotted three Huns very low down, but each time I dived they got under small banks of cloud and I lost them. Altogether, yesterday, I did about five hours flying.

This morning I did a line patrol with Romney. There was a strong west wind blowing and we were constantly being blown over the lines. There were high banks of cloud at about 6,000 feet and we climbed to 16,000. The effect was very wonderful from above.

But there was nothing doing. No Huns—not even 'Archie.'

I didn't go into details about the rag because I thought I had implied all there was to say.

Anyhow there were seven of us and we got there at 5.45 p.m., and sat in a café and drank cocktails until dinner time, and then had dinner!

Voila tout! Utterly unromantic, quite foolish, and yet I avow without apology that I found it very amusing at the time.

It was when we arrived back—a very noisy and irresponsible tenderful that the Odd Man declared he must come next time.

Whether to control or to join in the game was not quite clear.

Oh, more news! The 'air-hog' has just got an M.C. for general keenness and good work.

Our flight is 'standing by,' but I do not think we shall have another patrol.

This morning just before we got to the lines there was a big scrap in which our 'tripe-hounds'—as the facetious call the tri-planes—got two Huns and our two-seaters got one, but two of ours are missing.

It appears that the Hun sent over about twenty machines in one raid. They haven't been seen in the sky to-day apart from that.

I have seen some fellows of —— Squadron who told me that Fitz-Garrick's mother has had a letter from him from Germany.

I am wondering where you are at this moment. Wherever you are, I am always thinking of you and loving you. Whatever I am doing I think of you all the time.

Bien Aimée, I adore you.

All yours,

BILL.

P.S.—The letters I had to-day were the one written in the train and the one of the day following. I loved both, but particularly about your journey. I recalled our journeys together.

BILL."

Isn't he perfect? I think I will go out into the park and think about him.

  . . . .

In the park people were doing a church parade.

I sat under a parasol and watched them pass up and down in the sunshine. There were lots of women with new and very chic clothes, and there were soldiers with rows of ribbons. Those who had their "wings up" gave me a little pain in my heart, for I remember stitching the first pair to Bill's tunic. They had to be perfectly straight, you know, so it was more of a task than it might have been.

But I couldn't have allowed anyone else to do it, of course.

Then there were "The Creditors"—the maimed and blinded ones—some in bath chairs; some on crutches; some holding another by the arm for guidance.

They had young faces, and I wondered if they must move like that until time should make their faces old.

I would have liked to speak to them—to comfort myself by hearing that their spirits dismissed restraint though their feet no more could carry them swiftly where they chose to go.

I hoped too that each had found his woman and that each woman had kept faith.

"How marvellous," I thought, "would be the spiritual revelation of such a union, if the man were great enough to accept the love and service, and the women felt all joy in giving!"

. . . .

Someone spoke my name.

Dragging my mind from its abstraction, I looked—and there was Harvey leaning on his two rubber-capped sticks.

I stared without speaking for a moment or two, and then feebly said "Hullo!"

XXV

IT has been a warm and lovely evening. We dined in Piccadilly and afterwards came out into the gloaming to wander along under the deep sky.

Past the clubs overlooking the Green Park we went. Harvey, unwarlike in his conventional dinner clothes, but warlike enough in his disablement, stumped along on his sticks at my side.

It seemed so familiar; so much a repetition of what had been, that I felt obliged to remind myself all was not as before; that now, released from the feverish bondage which had enchained me, I could walk calmly, guarded by the security of my true love.

At last, contemplating the brown earth of the empty row, we paused.

At dinner the talk had been superficial, as it

is with two who have been intimate and between whom there is no more intimacy.

And during the walk we hadn't spoken; but now, abruptly, Harvey said:

"So you've solved the problem... your marriage is a success!"

For a while I had no reply. What is one to say to such a statement.

Whoever "solves the problem" and what is "success"?

Could I tell him, to whom ambition had seemed all important during the days when I would have given myself; given my body—and my mind, with its woman's capacity of which men have need though they may neither admit nor know it—that my marriage had taken me to an enchanted world?

I could tell him in a measure—and I did, in fairness to Bill... and myself.

Yet I had understood him so well.

His Destiny had given him his gods; those gods that mocked me to my utter desolation. Even war and his part in it had left them firmly rooted; and if, eager to escape, I had fled away at last, the fault was mine, not his.

My Destiny had led me to my garden—and the irony of it was that the gods fell as I turned to go. He was left alone outside without them—even without me! I had no wish—Oh, indeed, indeed I had no wish, for such a victory!

My hope now is that some other woman may come and guide him also into the place where truth is———.

.   .   .   .

Bill's letter of this morning—Monday—still says nothing of the proofs and the stupendous news about the book. Counting the posts again I know that even Tuesday may not bring his reply.

But the sight of his writing is sufficient to dwarf everything else.

> "'Cherie,' he begins.
>
> Another thrilling letter from you—the one written last Monday in the Park when you stayed there all day with the Babes.
>
> Both I and my pen are speechless over it. I cannot say anything adequate. You are my life.
>
> .   .   .   .
>
> More news of the 'Air Hog!'
> Last night he was seen to be hit— presumably by 'Archie.' His machine went down under control and crashed on the ground. This was about a mile behind the front line trenches.
>
> Several hours later the Odd Man was able to find him in a casualty station. He had a compound fracture of the right leg

and the left ankle was smashed up. He was quite conscious and could tell all about it.

His machine had been hit when he was flying low at about 4,500 feet. A gas attack and a big bombardment was on at the time.

The shell hit the engine and burst on percussion. It blew out part of the engine, tore off the under carriage and made a big hole in the bottom of the fuselage.

The 'Air Hog' was hit in the legs by fragments of shell. He found himself sitting in an open framework with one leg dangling down useless.

With the other, the left, although the ankle was smashed, he managed to steer. Though the balance was all wrong, he forced his machine down in a steady glide, avoided some trees and chose a clear place to land.

He crashed on landing, of course, but crawled out of the hole in front and was found by the ambulance men a few minutes later. He was perfectly conscious and never lost consciousness the whole time.

It was a wonderful performance and a miracle too, to have a direct hit and still be alive. He may be badly crippled, but he is in no serious danger.

No more 'jolly old patrols' for him, however!

.   .   .   .

I interrupted the writing of this to play a set of tennis. It is frightfully hot and I am sitting now on my bed with a long drink on the table beside me—white wine, lemon squash, and soda.

I am not due out on patrol until this evening, but before that I am going up to test my machine. The original engine has been taken out to be overhauled after doing nearly sixty hours, and a new engine is being put in.

Tell Babe the Second that I promise to write to her soon. The Golliwog she made still scouts for Huns.

.   .   .   .

I was glad about your decision not to see Harvey when in town. Yes, I think you could do no less than answer his letter.

Oh, my dearest woman, I love you. I send you all my most passionate vows.

BILL."

.   .   .   .

Reading those last words I wish that I had not dined with Harvey last night. I wouldn't care for Bill to dine with a woman who had kissed him before he knew me.

But at the moment it seemed to be making too much of it to refuse. The meeting of the morning was accidental too.

I hope the Air-Hog has a woman somewhere who will give thanks for his escape; for I think that among all this waste the least wasteful exits are made by those who leave no one to weep. Then one dies instead of two.

XXVI

THIS has come.

> "Dearest,
>
> Just a line to say I have submitted the proof to the C.O., but he has not returned it yet.
>
> In case it is used it must not be signed. I am sorry.
>
> I will write this evening at length.
>
> All yours,
>
> BILL."

Oh, I want his other letter quickly. I want to telephone to the man "upon whose advice one may rely" and tell him that everything can progress furiously.

Wait! Here is Purcell with a telegram. Now we can go ahead!

.   .   .   .

We can't go ahead!—The wire says "Permission refused!"

But this is impossible. There was *nothing—nothing*—in the proof to give "information" of any sort to the enemy. Why otherwise should permission be refused? This means that not only the articles but the book must be held over. And of what use will they be afterwards? Their whole value lies in the human appeal they would make to men and women at this very instant. How can I exist until to-morrow's letter comes?

.   .   .   .

It has come—the letter of explanation—but I am unconvinced. How could I be convinced with this:—

"My dearest One,
    I am sorry. The C.O. is afraid that the squadron would be too easily recognised, and I think the same.
    I don't know what to do now. We can only wait until I come home on leave.

Yesterday I did two patrols—the early one at 4.30 a.m. and the last at 7.30. There was nothing doing on either.

To-night we are having a special celebration dinner. Romney, who has been out here a long time, and has brought down many Huns, is going home to-morrow.

We expect he will get a squadron and his majority—in addition to his M.C., and Croix de Guerre.

He is an awfully dear fellow and absolutely the stoutest-hearted I have ever met. He is about 35 and married.

This morning I went up for a joy-ride and did an hour over the lines alone.

I hope you are not very depressed over the wash-out. I'm not—though I'm disappointed. We have *done* something in any case.

And I love you and I know you love me. Dear, dear one.

All yours,

BILL."

How could he—what does he mean by writing to me like that after all my striving?

It was my "bit"—the only thing I could do for him while he did his share.

I was so glad because I thought he would be overjoyed.

It was utterly wrong for him to agree with the C.O. What does a "tousle-headed youth in pyjamas" know of our career? Couldn't Bill have argued with him and explained that anything identifying the squadron to anyone, except the squadron itself, could be altered? But to leave it like that—just final!

And he doesn't seem to mind. I daren't write to him, I might say too much.

.   .   .   .

I did write yesterday after all, because I realised that I should be sorry afterwards to know that Bill didn't have a letter for each day.

I told him that I think he should have made some effort about this opportunity that will, perhaps, affect his and my whole future; but I don't think I expressed my amazement at his airy dismissal of it all. Now I hope I didn't, for it seems so trivial when one reads this:

"Ma Bien-Aimée,
    Your letter of last Thursday saying you have managed to do another short story has just come. I am glad about that, for you must be disappointed about the other 'wash out' after all your hard work.

.   .   .   .

Things have livened up again considerably. After writing you yesterday I went out on an escort job over X——. I am leading patrols now all the time and am temporarily in command of my flight.

We flew very high to protect a two-seater taking photos.

After it had finished and gone I spotted two Hun scouts going south. We chased them to X——, and then above five miles further east, but could not come up with them.

After tea I went out a third time with one other fellow. At 17,000 feet over X—— three Hun scouts appeared suddenly above me. I was very surprised, for the sky was thick with our own scouts, but they were all further west.

For a few minutes we kept our positions. Then the Huns came nearer until at last I pulled down my gun and fired up at the nearest, who was about 200 feet above me. He did a sudden turn, when I had fired about 25 rounds, and dived steeply away.

The others twisted and turned, and I thought they were going to dive on me, but a patrol of our scouts came up and the Huns sheered off.

Towards the end of the patrol when I was losing height, I saw four red Hun scouts below me and dived on the nearest.

(The other fellow with me I had lost. He had got mixed up in another formation.)

I fired twenty rounds at long range; and the whole four turned away!

This morning six of us, Kyrle leading one and I the other formation—had to escort six machines that were going for photos again. It turned out awfully well. The photo people led at about 11,000 and we were above and at either side slightly to the rear.

The poor leaders got smothered in 'Archie' bursts the whole time and we sailed along above in comfort.

At last, when a long way over, a formation of Hun scouts and two-seaters appeared to the north-west of us. The Huns didn't see us and went for the two-seaters; and seemed surprised when we dived into the middle of them.

I picked out a fat two-seater and put fifty rounds into him. He sent out clouds of smoke and fumes and started diving away. I couldn't watch it because for the next ten minutes we were in a swirl of Huns and ourselves, all tearing round and round and firing guns.

When finally we got into some sort of formation again all of us were there intact.

I climbed up again with one other

fellow following, to head off five Huns
who were coming up from the south, and
for twenty minutes we manoeuvred until
finally the Huns went too far over the
lines to follow.

We all got back, and I found that one
fellow had got one Hun down for certain.
All had had scraps at close quarters with
results not seen.

I had rather a 'head' last night when I
got down—after nearly three hours during
the day at over 16,000 feet. However, I
forgot all about it at dinner—our farewell
to Romney—and to-day I am quite fit
again.

·   ·   ·   ·

I forgot to tell you that the Air Hog had
to lose one leg below the knee. He is
getting on quite well though up to now.

I don't think many people have so well
won an M.C.

·   ·   ·   ·

Dearest, most precious one, I don't
want you to work so hard as you have
been doing—especially in town. You will
begin to look tired again.

Aimée, I love you.

BILL."

But, Bill dear, what are we women to do just now if we don't work "too hard"? How can we sit in idleness and think of the risks you take? Indeed, in that case we should look more than tired. There would be nothing left when you came to find us.

XXVII

HE "upon whose advice one may rely" thinks that the book will be of use afterwards, and that "Ad Astra" might, with advantage, preface it.

This will be good news to Bill and it is good news to me—but truly I admit my triviality.

What does a mere disappointment matter these days?

What does anything matter except that lovers should be re-united; and by lovers I think of them that love—mothers and children; husbands and wives; and those whose union is not recognised—all, all who love!

But yes, something matters more. It is that they who lose their lovers may not lose also Faith and Hope, and Charity.

Oh, there must be an afterwards. This can't be the End.

"Darling lover"—Bill says to-day.

"I cannot explain how anxious I am about your disappointment.

Your lovely letter which came this morning—written on Friday last, was so glowing with the thought of our success that it quite gave me a pain to think that by now you have my telegram and know we have come to a dead end—in that direction at any rate.

.   .   .   .

I think I got two Huns last night. It was on the last patrol again; it is becoming a regular thing to meet all the Huns just about sunset.

I led a formation of six and crossed the lines at 11,000 feet. When I turned down south I saw five Hun scouts about two miles away east and manoeuvred to approach them with the sun behind me.

The sun is absolutely blinding at sunset when you're in the sky.

I got quite close to the nearest one and fired 30 rounds at him. He and the others dived east straight away, and in turning west I lost sight of them.

But one of my patrol watched for several minutes the Hun I had fired at and saw him falling and fluttering about right to the ground, quite out control.

Twenty minutes later, when coming north again—all this was about six miles east of the lines—I saw a formation of red scouts. They were a long way below us, and I had also to go down indirectly to get the sun behind me again.

At last I did this and then went all out for the nearest one. There were seven of them. I got quite close again and finished my drum, zoomed out and climbed west again.

While changing the empty drum for a full one I looked around and saw the Hun I had tackled slowly stall, stand upright, and then fall down sideways; sometimes he spun, sometimes dived. I must have got him too.

Having a full drum on the gun again I went back. I could see the various ones of my patrol diving on to the red scouts. I chose, as I thought, the nearest Hun and started firing. The gun stopped after one shot.

But as I reached up to clear the stoppage I heard the horrid noise of a Hun's double gun just behind me.

I hadn't chosen the nearest Hun after all, but had passed one; and now he was on my tail.

I spun; the horrid noise stopped, so I stopped spinning.

Instantly the horrid noise started again.

I spun again. Once more the noise stopped and gently I eased my machine out of the spin and the dive.

But the Hun was still there.

When I heard the noise a third time I simply shut off the engine and *fell* down.

I had started scrapping at 12,000. I ventured to pull out level at 7,000.

Afterwards I learned that a scout of another squadron had dived on the Hun on my tail and had shot him down.

My machine wasn't hit anywhere. I didn't stay still long enough, I suppose.

Out of the seven red scouts another squadron got two and I got one—the others of my patrol didn't all get there in time to scrap, but they saw my first one fluttering.

To-day is 'dud'; the first 'dud' day since I saw Dick nearly a fortnight ago.

Au revoir, my sweet woman.

I am all yours,

BILL."

Two Huns within a few minutes! Well, as he is there for that purpose I suppose the more he gets the sooner the purpose will cease; but I can't be persuaded that because some wives were born in Hun-land they wait less anxiously for each post—that the sight of a telegram has less power to stab their hearts!

I believe that, however it is spelt, anguish must mean the same thing. Yes, I think of the wives always. May their gods give *them* Faith and Hope and Charity.

XXVIII

MOLLY has forwarded a letter from an old man I know. He says, "....I have searched my motor-map and Bradshaw for your whereabouts. What a Saxon nest for her for whom I invented an Egyptian classical name!"

You see it pleases him to be facetious at my expense, but he does it in the form of flattery, and that is why I wonder he escaped marriage.

I like to think that he has been very true to someone, who was taken away. But I'm a sentimentalist now-a-days, am I not?

Last night, in answer, I telephoned to say I had left my "Saxon nest" for a while; and to-night, at his flat, we dined together, for I refused his offer of "other guests". Other guests are all very well when you have had your say;

but I wanted to bring our friendship up to date.

The dinner was perfect and the atmosphere so rare in its austere sincerity. Certainly the servant, who, at that table, hands one the most delicious food, is not quite so aged as my host, but his courtesy is equal.

To celebrate my marriage we drank champagne. I liked it.

Afterwards, over our coffee and cigar and cigarette, we discussed music, and my host's work on war-hospital committees, and Bill; and we gossiped too, without malice, about people known to both of us.

Then I asked him to come and refresh himself with a sight of our lovely Downs.

At his age he should sit in a garden, under God's own Heaven, instead of wallowing in the smoke and grime of cities—but he refused, pleading his hospital duties.

I imagine he feels the absolute necessity for activity. He knows rest must come soon enough maybe!

.   .   .   .

Bill said this morning:

"Darling,
    Another of those, fortunately, rare days when no letter has come from you. All the

post brought was a letter from Dick. He says:

'What a sensation you made.... They are still talking about it in the Battery. It was a fine exhibition.'

Darling, I *do* wish I could show you too, because you can't imagine how beautiful my machine looks stunting and flashing in the sun.

There was nothing doing all day yesterday, and after the early patrol this morning the clouds came down low again. But now it is clearer and I expect I shall be out to-night. In any case if there is no patrol I shall go out on the range.

The day after you should receive this you will be travelling to the country again. I would like to be there in your room when you get back to it.

Oh, dearest one, to be near you.... I love you, my wife.

All yours,

BILL."

I can't bear it.... I can't bear it.... I want him to be there, in my room, waiting for me!

·   ·   ·   ·

We have come to the "Saxon Nest" again;

but neither Molly nor Nanny nor the family of one are here.

Their plan is to make a round of visits; and so that this house may not become too wrapped up in its own reflections, I have brought The Babes.

We have no maid.

One of the seven—or is it nine?—wonders of the world comes in the early morning to light the kitchen fire and clean everything to spotlessness. Afterwards she goes back to her cottage to cope with the necessities of four small children—which means cooking and cleaning, and cleaning and cooking. She grows her own vegetables too, and works in the fields and does all the washing and ironing for this household besides the flannels from the vicarage.

She never appears to hurry, nor to be tired, and her personal cleanliness is overwhelming. Her second husband is "at the war," and another child has a small grave in the churchyard here.

There's a life for you!

The Babes are enraptured. Each has her room, which she keeps tidy; and we all make our own beds.

Then we cook too.

I don't know why we were expected to know that cornflour must be mixed in cold milk before being added to the hot milk.

We know now.

Then I would have you bear in mind that raw meat doesn't keep, although the butcher calls only twice a week.

The smell was horrible. The seventh or ninth wonder removed it and gave a short, crisp lecture on "partial cooking."

We grow wiser each day. Soon I shall be fitted to call myself a wife.

Yesterday afternoon, on the Downs, Betty helped me to boil a kettle, while Bey romped about without a stitch of clothing on except a shady panama hat. The sun loved her body and poured down his warmth upon her.

This is how we boiled our kettle. Before starting, into an empty syrup tin we poured a very small amount of paraffin oil and a salt-spoonful of salt. Then when we wanted our stove we uncovered and placed it in a hollow of stones piled a little higher than itself so that a draught could wander between it and the kettle. Into the paraffin we dropped a lighted fir cone. Two or three times the flame went out and we had to fish for the cone and re-light it, but at length it blazed and the kettle boiled immediately. The salt, while keeping the paraffin from lighting so easily, prevents it burning away at once.

Our wisdom was not our own. We learnt it at

the vicarage while consuming an enormous tea the day before.

Betty said afterwards that probably they thought we had had no lunch, which wasn't exactly true—but nearly. The meat episode had taken place during the morning, you see.

.　.　.　.

This letter of Bill's is too wonderful. It makes me ache with desire for him.

> "My dearest dearest one,
> The blank of yesterday was filled to-day by your two lovely letters of Saturday and Sunday.
> Aimée, my dear wife, all your wonderings and questionings thrill me beyond words; certainly beyond written words. Were I close to you my first answer would be to kiss you till you could not breathe.
> But I can't put down on paper all that I would say. This I can say: that I am amazed all the time at the miracle of our marriage; amazed at finding myself capable of the richest love, for I have no reservations of which I am conscious; I am all yours and I want to deserve all you.
> I am amazed and thrilled that so deeply tender and passionate a love should bring

me such sanity and clearness in my mental attitude to you. I live only for you, my wife. I am utterly yours.

. . . .

By now you will have written to me after hearing that the Book and 'Daily ——' articles can't go on.

In a short time now—the time we dare not speak of—we'll be able to put our heads together and make something, from the material, with which we shall have no difficulty.

. . . .

Last night I started out on a line patrol, but the clouds were so thick that I got lost and came down 2,000 feet over the trenches.

I had only the 'Hun' with me—his first time over the lines. He was quite delighted because he saw a real Hun soldier in the trenches.

This morning we were up at 4.45, but the clouds were too low, so we went back to bed.

Later I went to the range, but when I started firing my gun didn't jam. On the contrary it wouldn't stop firing!

I scattered about 90 rounds over the

country side and came back to strafe the gun-room.

This evening I am due out on an O.P.

.   .   .   .

I don't know if I told you about our contour chasing.

The Squadron has gone quite mad over it. Nearly always on returning from patrol we come down low and chase around the roads and the camps about fifty feet off the ground. It is quite amusing and some funny things happen.

One fellow saw a band giving a concert one evening. He was about 300 feet high. Opening out his engine to produce its full noise he spiralled down directly over their heads.

For some moments nothing happened, and then he saw the conductor—a fat man—fling down his baton and throw up his arms in despair. The bandmen could not hear themselves play!

There was a big crowd of Tommies there, and as the machine zoomed up again they cheered and laughed and waved their caps, and the pilot laughed so much that he couldn't fly straight.

Doesn't sound fair, does it? However, the infantry still has a wonderfully good opinion of us.

I am going to the range now when I have posted this to you.

All my most passionate love,

BILL."

Aren't all men babes?

I think it is well that in the midst of death they can laugh so easily at life!

XXIX

Betty and I are cooks!

I used to think those who could turn raw flour and other raw things into something one liked to eat must have a special gift. Now I no longer am surprised, except that anyone should go on doing it day after day. We enjoyed ourselves because it was adventure; but I shouldn't care to be obliged to spend my time in a kitchen—even such a darling of a kitchen as this—whether I felt inclined or otherwise.

Our cakes are perfect, and the cornflour jelly stuff slips down like a dream. That's because it was flavoured with chocolate and had the beaten white of eggs stirred in at the last minute.

Prunes and rhubarb simply cook themselves

while you fold your hands and sit on the kitchen table. I did so and re-read my letter from Bill.

"My darling,

We are nearly sure that the enclosed cutting describes the scraps we had several days ago. Refer to my letter and see how nearly like it that is.

In some details it varies but not in much.

Then, again, the last paragraph obviously refers to the 'Air Hog'—except that he never lost consciousness.

I loved your letter of Monday, which I got at lunch to-day. I love your 'moods,' too. And you see how gravely I take them?

My dear, my dear, when we love we trust and understand, and we treasure all each other's quaintnesses. I love you always and am all yours.

. . . . .

Later.

The flight got two Huns to-day. The new flight commander Allison got one and Grahaeme, who is generally in my patrol, got the other.

It was on our return from escorting six two-seaters. Four Hun machines actually were over our side of the lines and Allison and Grahaeme climbed up while on the east of them and shot one each from underneath.

Grahaeme's was confirmed from the ground. It was seen to fall in the lines.

To-day I got your first letter, written after knowing of the C.O.'s refusal.

I am just as sick about it as you are, dearest one. Don't, please, think I approve the C.O. *refusing*; but, all the same, I had to agree with what he said.

It is the rigid etiquette of the R.F.C. that individually, squadrons and pilots should not be mentioned. (Ball is the solitary exception.) The C.O. said the squadron would be recognised. I couldn't deny that.

But, anyhow, right or wrong, having so much more vital daily work to do, I simply cannot even argue with him over this now. When I get to England I must try to arrange something with you.

I am sorry, so sorry, my dearest, to think of all your work and your hopes standing by for such a flimsy reason. Please do not be too much disappointed. Wait a little.

Darling, you are so intensely precious to me. I love you and want you just frightfully.

All my love,

BILL."

. . . .

To-day I should loathe to cook. I have a "head." It's the one Bill had the other day and it has just travelled across. For that reason I welcome it—but I'm glad I don't have to cook!

There is enough food in the pantry to satisfy the appetites of Betty and Bey, and I shall live on tea and and cigarettes for the next few hours.

That sounds like asking for trouble, doesn't it; but if you obey your instinct in these things you can't go wrong. Some "heads" wouldn't tolerate tea or cigarettes—and some will! Mine is the second sort.

Bill's letter is a tonic, though.

"Darling one," I read.

You are settled again in the country now I suppose, and with The Babes. My longing to be with you grows more intense.

I love you with all my life, bien-Aimée.

.   .   .   .

Yesterday morning one of our pilots was wounded. He had been here only three weeks and has done awfully well.

When he was wounded he was attacking a two-seater and was underneath it. The observer stood up and fired down on him and he was hit in the hip joint.

He came home and made a good landing, but is rather bad for he lost a lot of blood.

This morning Grahaeme went missing. He was out with Captain Allison and they got separated in the clouds. We may hear yet that he is down on this side, but there is a gale blowing from the west and we think he must be on the other side.

I did a line patrol last night and an O.P. this morning. But saw little. There were a few odd Huns about, but they stayed too far over east for us to dare to follow them in view of the gale from the west.

Later.

Grahaeme has just telephoned. He got mixed up in a big scrap and drifted a long way over the lines, lost his bearings, and landed finally at another aerodrome.

The mail is in, but there is no letter from you—only one from Joan. She says Dad spoke to you on the telephone last Wednesday.

I wish I could do that. My dearest, I long to hear your voice again.

.   .   .   .

I have just developed a very bad failing as a pilot. I have started landing badly.

The last dozen times I have returned to the aerodrome I have made simply awful exhibitions, and as these on several occasions followed a stunting show over the sheds they were quite humiliating.

This morning I broke my tail skid—tore it clean off. That makes the fifth I have smashed. I know why I land badly—afterwards. But I never know at the moment. It is a question only of tenths of a second. However, I will get it right again soon.

I did some shooting at the range yesterday. Going much nearer the ground, doing one quick short dive, and firing perhaps ten shots is, I find, much better than a long dive firing all the time.

I did either eight or nine dives, and the early ones were long ones. Towards the end I did short dives and the result showed the difference. In the last four dives I scored one, two, one and three hits respectively. The last was quite good, for I had only five rounds left when I started the dive. But I got so near that I nearly touched the ground, then fired and zoomed.

When you are scrapping with a Hun the same thing happens. The Hun is moving as well as you, and frequently towards you, that you touch almost before you fire.

In haste to catch the post. It goes in a minute.

All yours.

BILL."

XXX

THE old postman arrived to-day before I wakened properly.

Bey must have seen him come up the path for, half consciously, I heard her scamper down; then clad in her small kimono and bedroom slippers she tip-toed into my room determined not to rouse me, I suppose. Unable to resist temptation, however, she spent the next few minutes labouring to balance something on my nose. Knowing what was expected of me I slept soundly until this was achieved, and she had, with muffled giggles and gurgles, tip-toed carefully away.

Then I opened my eyes and read:—

"My wonderful lover,
    Three letters from you to-day—one written in town, the last from there; one in the train, and one from the country. Darling, I am frantically happy.

To-day the Odd Man received the June issue of his magazine, in which appears my article. I enclose it.

On the whole, I think it is rather good; don't you?

This morning I was called at 3.30 by the C.O. to go for a special stunt. For four days running a Hun, greatly daring, has come over the aerodrome just after day-break.

The C.O. proposed last night that we should leave the ground the moment it was light if the clouds permitted, and try to catch him.

We got off the ground at 4 a.m.—a few minutes before in fact. We climbed to 18,500 feet over the aerodrome and watched for signals from the ground.

But no Hun came. Anyhow it was a lovely morning and, apart from the frozen fingers, I enjoyed the flip. We finished by patrolling the line for three-quarters of an hour and then came contour chasing home.

I was out again at 9.30 on another escort to two-seaters, who were taking photographs.

This afternoon I played tennis, and tonight I lead an O.P. at seven o'clock.

I expect to get another letter from you to-morrow. My dear one, I love your letters; they mean more to me than I dare say or think. I love you more every day, every minute.

All yours.

BILL.

P.S.—You are my *wife* you know!"

After reading this—feeling very glad about myself and Bill, I rose and went down into the stone-flagged kitchen, where the seventh or ninth wonder had left a bright fire burning. The kettle sang and the double saucepan waited for the porridge which I mixed so that it neither would be thick nor thin—then set it on the stove and came up to bathe and dress.

Bey already had bathed herself and was hurrying into her scanty clothing so that she might have time to play with the kittens in the sunshine of the garden before breakfast. Betty, who likes her sleep in solid chunks, called lazily for me to run her water when I'd let my own away.

And so about nine o'clock we sat down to breakfast, in the nursery that, like every other room in the house, is as cheerful as it is simple and picturesque.

Later, after preparing the mid-day meal, I went for the cream, which means a walk of four miles altogether. And these, as nearly as I can recall, were my thoughts:

"I hope The Babes will be all right playing in the garden alone.... They ought to be.... Betty is old enough now.... Bill's letter is so sweet.... I wish he were here.... Wouldn't it be too wonderful to have him.... I wonder what he is doing at this moment.... It's hardly worth while coming all this way for cream when it's so hot—but then it's so good for growing children. I wish our own milk people didn't make all theirs into butter.... Let me see, I mustn't forget to let Bill know that they had written from the 'Daily ——' about his articles.... I'll say he might at least have taken the trouble to write to them, especially as I asked him to.... No, I won't say that.... I should be dreadfully sorry afterwards. I'll say I thought he had done so and that I didn't because I loathed having to refuse the chance.... Let me think—if I were to beat some of the cream very stiff, would it disguise the milk pudding enough to make The Babes not realise what they were eating? It's so good for them.... Oh, I mustn't forget to add some white of egg.... I remember the book said that.... I feel certain Bill could have argued with the C.O. about those articles!... I should have done so.... I'm surprised he didn't bother even though he—what *shall* I do with the yoke of

that egg.... It mustn't be wasted and I don't
want it for anything.... I know.... I'll
swallow it whole and let Betty and Bey
watch me.... They'll love that. Bey will
shriek with mirth.... Yes, I'll tell Bill that I
didn't think much of the article he did for
the Odd Man's magazine... it wasn't a bit
vivid.... Not on the same plane as his letters
to me. I shall enjoy telling him.... He was
rather bucked with it too.... Now if that
chicken is to be hot for Sunday's dinner I can't
possibly go to church.... How can I?...
And if I don't the Babes won't—and we
didn't go last Sunday. The village mothers
don't go because they have the meal to
cook. But they send their children. I'm sure
Betty and Bey would not be sent—besides
I'm not their mother! I quite forgot to ask
the price of the chicken.... Goodness, I
remember the woman on Salisbury Plain
said they'd be worth their weight in gold.
I hope this one isn't... we haven't enough
money in the house, nor in the bank
either!... It'll be fearfully exciting cooking
it. I hope Betty and Bey won't get too hot
rushing about.... Bey's tummy *is* rather
out of proportion to her size, ...but I
suppose it's all right.... All small children
have large tummies. It's where they keep
their extra nourishment, I expect.... I think

I'll ask the grocer man if he...."

You see what it is to be a housewife? I must pull myself together, mustn't I?

XXXI

"MY own wife,

We had a quaint patrol last night. All the flight did it. Allison led one patrol of three and I led the other. One fellow dropped out, however, and five of us crossed the lines.

We soon saw seven Hun scouts leave their aerodrome and start climbing away from us.

Hoping to entice them to the lines, Allison turned west and re-crossed the trenches. We turned south, climbed hard for twenty minutes, and crossed again.

We were at 16,000 feet when we saw the Huns about 2,000 feet below us. There were, roughly, a dozen of them—all scouts and wonderfully painted. No two were alike, and hardly one machine was painted all the same colour. Green wings and red fuselage; pink and purple; yellow tails and white and black wings! They were hideous.

We had been in formation, but when we saw the Huns and Allison started twisting about to get into position, two of our pilots lost height and got underneath him.

I closed up to him, with Grahaeme close on me and the three of us tore round and round, like a circus—each on the other's tail.

Allison was looking for four of us and could see only two.

Below us the Huns were going round and round also, but in the greatest confusion. It was screamingly funny. I don't think we were really happy—so few against a dozen and a dozen miles east of the lines—but the Huns were less happy.

First one and then the other would get out of control and start spinning, dive, and flatten out and climb up again. They had the wind up, all right!

Well we continued this round-about business for five minutes, and I wondered when the leader was going to dive. I wondered also how we should get back such a distance to the lines if we lost height and got mixed up with the Huns.

At last Allison decided apparently that

it was not good enough and he turned away west.

Ultimately we got into formation again. When we got home we had been out two hours and five minutes and had each only a few pints of petrol left.

It was really the better course not to have had a scrap under all the conditions, though perhaps we might have tried just one dive each and tootled home promptly afterwards.

.   .   .   .

I didn't tell you about my fifteen minutes' battle the other day.

I was out on an O.P. with one other fellow—the third had gone back with engine trouble—and when east of the trenches I saw a lot of English 'Archie' bursts to westward. A moment afterwards I spotted a machine making for the lines. We were at 15,000 feet and the other machine at 12,000.

I immediately dived a bit to head him off. He turned north and I turned north, too, to get in front of him. He turned south and the other fellow headed him off. Then he came east climbing. I climbed west, and he gave it up.

At last he put his nose down and came

due east to pass under me. I dived straight for him, with my eye on the gun sights and the Hun at the other end of them and my finger on the trigger lever.... Then.... the Venetian blind effect appeared and I saw it was a tri-plane— one of our own machines!

Either it had been 'Archied' by mistake, or there was a real Hun further west that I could not see.

To-day I had your letter written in the garden on Friday.

I have just run out of paper of the size I usually use, but I can love you just as much on this as on any other—and I do.

All my love, my sweet wife,

BILL."

.　　.　　.　　.

We have had an Event!

Just now—keeping a motherly eye on Bey while she cleaned her teeth—suddenly I heard Betty shriek from her room:

"Cows—cows. Oh, cows!"

Her voice carried all the shrill notes of excitement and I could hear her darting about.

"What is it?... What do you mean?" I called back, and Bey demanded in her curiously deep and impatient tones:

"What is it on earf?"

"That's not the way to speak, darling," I dutifully began, while Betty came running, clothed in her undergarments, hair brush in hand.

"There's millions of cows in the garden," she panted .... "Crowds and crowds, and they're rushing furiously about, on the lawn—all going mad!"

Allowing for the exaggeration usual to females of Betty's age there remained a possibility of cows in the garden; so, as Bey ran out after her, I followed from the bathroom to the bedroom window—and there truly were the herd.

They seemed to be panic stricken—drifting sometimes; sometimes tearing in confusion, sometimes standing for a second and then leaping grotesquely.

The three of us watched, our heads all out of the one casement, and our breath coming in jerks to match the antics of the cattle.

By and by the shadow of a human being detached itself from the meadow beyond.

It was weird and unreal in the gloaming, so that I scarcely could find my voice to call out and ask the meaning of what was happening. And when I did call, the head of the shadow tilted upward as though to discover us, but no answer came.

Away, beyond, the circle of the Downs

looked black and rather terrible. One pure white animal, frantically leaping, seemed ghostly in the dusk. It crossed my mind how dreadful a stampede of untamed beasts must be;—the thud, thud of the hoofs of living things out of gear; the unreasonable infection of the panic; the horrible turmoil of the uncontrolled; the uncontrollable!

I pictured being down there, petrified, in their midst, while they trampled hideously about.

At last these real and harmless creatures gathered together in some sort of order and trotted out of the opening into their own country.

Then I realised that Bey ran a risk of pneumonia. Already she had been late, too, owing to the misdemeanour of Cotton-tail who had hidden herself in the hedge.

So I bustled this babe into her "nighty" while she hopped about, ... sizzling with the after-effects of the event. Soon she lay, looking too angelic in her narrow white bed under the pale blue coverlet.

"Good-night, sweet," I said, "sleep well."

She pulled down my head and kissed me fervently.

"G'night.... G'night," she breathed, "an' ha'nt it been an ab-fo-lutely *wond*-o-ful tweat!"

I arranged the tall screen on which storks fly about to greet her in the morning; and leaving the casement wide open to the tender air I went from the room carrying my flickering candle carefully.

"If a few cows in the wrong place at the wrong time provide one babe with an 'absolutely wonderful treat,' another babe with the pitch of excitement, and one grown-up woman with reflections on the uncanny, why, surely, life's a simple problem after all," I thought.

.　　.　　.　　.

I came to my room and drew the curtains across to hide the night. It was beautiful, but too sad for me. Bill's letter lay on the table— the one important thing in the muddle of books and papers and writing materials. I sat down and looked at it; then I took it from the envelope to read again. It was less likely than many to soothe a rebellious tendency.

"Dear, dear Aimée,
We had the hell of a scrap last night. It was the sequel to the encounter of the previous evening which I described yesterday. Allison proposed that we should go out and look for the same crowd of Huns again. So six of us started, with Allison leading, and we crossed the lines and

worked down south, well over on the Hun side, before two fellows had to go back with dud engines.

At last we came up to the Huns. I saw four about 2,000 feet below us, and then five further east and above us.

I don't know whether Allison saw those above us or not. However it was, he dived vertically on the nearest Hun and I dived just behind him and went for the second.

As I was going down on to mine I could see Allison close with his; then saw the Hun go down spinning, with engine full on, in a violent spiral. There was no room for doubt as to whether the Hun was hit.

Most of this I saw semi-consciously, for I was sighting on to my Hun. I got very close and fired 30 or 40 rounds while he was flying level. Then when I almost collided with him, he dived. I followed and finished the drum and zoomed out.

I turned west and climbed hard, but the other two fellows apparently kept the Huns busy, for none followed me. I proceeded with changing my drum and watched the Hun I had attacked still diving, not very steeply, but going directly west! I was then about 9,000 feet. We had all come down in the world a lot—and finally I saw the Hun crash in the ground among some patches of swamp.

Having changed my drum and climbed to 11,000 I turned east again and saw the scrap still going on.

I headed for them again and got in a burst of 25 rounds at another Albatross. He dived out of my sights and the same instant two Huns dived on me. They were almost directly above me, and I could only dive for all I was worth. They followed me to the lines, and by that time I had lost 7,000 feet.

.   .   .   .

It was practically dark when I landed. I was the last one home. Allison had not arrived, and nothing has been heard of him since.

The other two of our four had started to follow us down, but had the high Huns on them immediately. They had had quite a struggle and had been shot about a bit.

They had both seen Allison and me, however, close in with a Hun each, and both are certain the two were brought down.

I had one bullet through my right plane.

The Colonel of the wing came over this morning to ask me all about it. We are

sorry Allison did not get back. He was
such an excellent patrol leader.

The post goes in a minute. I love you,
sweetest one, and am all yours.

BILL."

I am no philosopher to-night.

XXXII

"Midnight, Wednesday.

Darling,

I did not fly all to-day. We were
standing by most of the time, and in the
evening I was to have led nine machines
on the same quest as the previous evening,
but about tea time a thunderstorm came
on and the whole thing was washed out.

To-day makes exactly two months
since I arrived at the squadron—56 days.
Up to yesterday I have done 135 hours
flying—or 108 with the squadron here.
There have been many changes since I
came—five have gone missing, two
wounded, two crashed, six gone sick, and
two gone home at the end of their time—

which makes seventeen that have left the squadron since I came.

Now I am ninth on the list in order of arrival—that is, eight of the seventeen who have been struck off were here before me, and the others have arrived after me.

It really is remarkable how, in every squadron, most of the people who are missing are new arrivals. All five from here arrived after me.

To-morrow I get up at 5 a.m. to do a bombing escort, so I will finish this at midday (this is the second letter I have written you to-day) when the post has come in.

Good-night, dearest one.

BILL."

Today the papers are full of the new "advance."

Heaven above, what that means! What a fever of emotion—of physical and mental delirium. I hold my letter in my hand, but before I open it I say my prayer for the wives who have no letter from their lovers to-day.

I say my prayer for them—though to whom I pray I do not know.

Thursday, 2 p.m.

"My dear, dear wife,

I was thrilled to ecstacy by your letter

which came this morning—the one written
on Sunday telling me of your love. I am
amazed with the wonder and completeness
of it all. Bien-Aimée, I worship you, in all
your moods, just all the time.

.   .   .   .

By the time you get this the news of
another great battle will be several days
old to you.

It started this morning—out of our
area, but we started too. At 5.45 I was off
the ground with seven machines to escort
the bomb raid I mentioned last night.

When we got up past B—— we saw
the battle burning. It was wonderful to be
able to see it all like that; but, oh, it is so
stupid and senseless. A patch of country
about twenty miles long and twelve miles
deep was just ablaze.

The 'push' had started at 3.45 a.m., and
already at 6 a.m. the artillery barrage had
moved forward several miles, leaving a
smoking, churned, shell-pocked brown
belt of destroyed country behind it.

To the west of, and right up to the
original line of trenches, the whole of the
fields and woods and roads were livid with
the flashes of our guns—not just a dart of

flame here and one there, but a dancing, pricking, shimmering mass of heat.

Towards the eastern edge of the smoking belt was a constant band of white shrapnel bursts, like snowdrops overcrowded in a garden border, and before them and behind them and on both sides of them the continuous eruptions of red earth and dust where the increasing rain of high explosive shells was falling!

.   .   .   .

I flew over this, 12,000 feet above it, and thanked some of my gods that I was no longer a landsman in combat.

.   .   .   .

The Squadron has done remarkably well at the start of the big push. Four Huns on two patrols. But one of our machines is missing—at least he is two hours overdue.

When the bombers were dropping their bombs and we were looking on this morning, three foolish Hun scouts dropped out of the clouds into the midst of us. One got on my tail—I was quite unconscious of it—and Grahaeme promptly filled him with over 80 rounds. He went down and was seen by two other pilots to crash. A second Hun was shot down before he saw us.

The third flew level with me just for an instant, and then dived below me. I turned more quickly than he had done and dived vertically at him and fired 20 rounds. He continued to dive and got out of decent range, so I climbed up to the formation again and we handed back the bombing machines safely across the lines.

We were all intact, too.

The wing commander came round about noon and was fearfully pleased with our start. While he was there the Brigadier turned up, too, and was hearing all about it when six of a second patrol of seven returned with a claim of two Huns certain and perhaps others.

The squadron is rather pleased with itself!

Now this afternoon, it is appallingly warm, but there's no work for us until after tea. Then I may take a patrol about 6 p.m. and finish for the day.

Your picture of Babe the second is very sweet. I have one, particularly intimate, of you, which is so sweet!

I love you.

BILL."

Do listen to this!

I never knew anyone so adaptable as Bill. Equally he can appreciate the Odd Man's point of view and the inability of Grahaeme to express himself as the Odd Man would wish.

I think it is priceless to be able to put yourself in everyone's place. He is teaching me that lesson among many others.

Friday, 2nd.

"My dearest woman.

Another sweet letter from you written last Monday on the Downs.

As I felt when I first came out, so I feel now—how wonderful it is to have someone who matters so much to me; who gives me inspiration to live.

Aimée darling!

The weather turned 'dud' yesterday afternoon, so I had no further work to do. I was down for a patrol at 8 this morning too, but the clouds came over and I am still standing by.

I've mentioned Grahaeme several times, haven't I? He's my right hand man on patrol and is wonderfully reliable.

He's a Canadian and talks it violently and nasally—when he does talk, which is rare. Usually he is very quiet.

But when he is excited—say, when he comes back from a scrap—nothing holds him. His language, all unconsciously, is lurid. And as it generally happens that the Odd Man is waiting to know all about it, the result is thrilling.

'Anything doing?' says the Odd Man.

'Why, Christ Almighty, I should say there was!' shouts Grahaeme. He has still his helmet on, and as he can't hear well he thinks he has to shout. He goes on—'The sky's stiff with bloody Huns.'

The Odd Man does not continue for the moment, but just looks thoughtful. Someone else, less sensitive to blasphemy, goes on with the interrogation until the Odd Man, forgetting his feelings in the excitement of the story, chips in again.

'Did you get one down?'

'Jesus, yes! There were three of them red b—s— and I was diving on one when I heard someone pooping at me with his —It isn't only on these occasions that — —double gun.... "Hell!" I said. "There's another damned Hun on my tail." So I yanked up the old 'bus and got on the devil's tail instead and just pumped blue hell into him!... Christ—away he went spinning to hell and gone!"

No comment from the Odd Man!

It isn't only on these occasions that Grahaeme's mode of expression is unusual.

At breakfast this morning the Odd Man was seated next to him and said:

'Out for more Huns to-day, Grahaeme?'

'Jesus, yes!' said Grahaeme fervently and quite gravely.

'Well, it's quite the right spirit anyway,' commented the Odd Man in the stifled silence.

.   .   .   .

The fellow missing yesterday was one of the second patrol. He was fairly experienced but not on scouts.

Someone in the squadron has heard from Hyatt. His memory is not normal yet, and he is still in hospital. The 'Air Hog' is in London now and is getting on well.

I send you all my love, dear one.

BILL."

Saturday, 2.30.

"Dear, dear woman,

It was such a tiny letter from you to-day, but so very sweet because you love me and I adore you.

A short note came from Dick too, saying he had received my letter by aerial post.

.   .   .   .

I have just reckoned up my scraps and

find I have got four certain, four probable, and one balloon (which is counted two Huns), total 10 (not out).

My note will be short as there is no very thrilling news. Though the strafe is tremendous and still goes on we are getting only one job a day.

I was out this morning at 5.30 a.m., but did not cross the lines. The clouds were down too low.

I went up the lines and saw all the progress that has been made. It is very decided.

All my love,

BILL.

P.S.—The last R.F.C. communiqué says:
'Lieut. G—— and Lieut. B—— (me), of —— squadron, engaged a hostile formation of five scouts and drove one down obviously out of control; and on the same patrol Lieut. B—— attacked seven H.A. and shot one down.'

This morning I wakened and looked at my watch. It was nine o'clock. At twenty minutes past nine the taxi was coming to take Mother to the station five miles away! She had been persuaded, much to her surprise, to come for a week-end, and in spite of her denial

I knew she was pining to find herself back in town.

I leapt from bed and, without waiting to slip into my kimono, ran into Bey's room. She slept soundly.

As, usually, she rises soon after the birds, I thought the hands of my watch must have grown tired of going round and round, and had run races in the night; but, reaching the day nursery, I saw that the clock there said a minute past nine! I tore into the kitchen to find that the seventh or ninth wonder had been more wonderful than ever, for the kettles had reached boiling point at that very moment. Speedily I made tea, cut bread and butter and carried it all up to Mother's room. She lay asleep.

" Your taxi comes in a quarter of an hour," I cried callously. "Get up.... Get up, or you'll have to stay here another day!"

That roused her. She opened her eyes wide.

"What!" she cried.

"It's five past nine," I said. "We've all overslept."

I was pouring the tea as I spoke; then I missed something.

"The letters!" I exclaimed. "I wonder where they are?"

Leaving Mother staring blankly at the cup in her hand I raced down again, but could find no sign of letters either in the door or outside, where I had directed the old man to leave them if we didn't answer at any time.

Slowly I climbed the stairs.

Yesterday, Monday, there had been no letter from Bill; and when that happens, as a rule two are delivered on Tuesday.

I didn't like the morning any more.

But there was Mother to be seen to, so I went back to her room.

"What does Bill say?" she asked—still sleepily.

"I don't know.... There's no letter," I replied.

And then I heard the gate click and, glancing out of the window, saw old Mrs. Witchell hobbling up the path with her hands full of envelopes. I shall love her evermore.

.   .   .   .   .

There were seven for me—three of them from Bill.

While Mother dressed, vaguely I read the other four—making comments all the while.

"But what has Bill got to say?" she insisted.

"I don't know," I said again, but added this time, "I like to keep his letters until I'm alone in my room."

At this she said nothing but looked disappointed, and I knew she was curious to hear the latest news.

"I'll open the last one," I conceded, breaking the flap apart as I spoke.

It was short—one tiny page torn from a notebook. It said:

> *"Saturday, 4.20 a.m.*
> Just got this; all unexpected! But I still love you.
> Darling, it intensifies my delight a thousand times to have you this time to tell the news.
> All yours, bar and all.
>
> BILL."

I stared at it. A pink slip fell from the envelope on to my knee. It was separated into little oblong squares like a telegraph form— each word having a box of its own. My eyes gazed, then I understood.

"Oh, Mummy," I cried, "Bill has got a bar to his M.C.!"

. . . . .

Soon afterwards the taxi appeared. Bey had wakened and came along the passage in her small blue kimono, squashing the black cat in her arms.

"What's all happening?" she asked.... "Why's Mumsie up?"

"We've slept late, darling... and the taxi's waiting... and Bill's got a bar to his M.C.," I cried.

"Good ol' Bill," she murmured.... "Lie still, puff-puff!... Mumsie don't go back to nasty ol' town.... Stay wif us here!"

.   .   .   .

We got Mother off at last.

Bey went to the gate, and Betty, who ran out of her room at the last minute, hung with me from the window.

"Don't forget to change," I called.... "And it's the *other* side of the platform!"

"And don't forget to get out at the end," giggled Betty hilariously.

"G'bye, Mumsie.... An' don't forget an' leave you' specackles in ve twain," we heard Bey shout.

Then the engine of the taxi gathered speed and over the hedge we caught glimpses of the top of Mother's head, and a waving handkerchief.

"I hope she won't take the wrong train," I said.

"She's sure to," dismissed Betty casually as she lifted the lid from the teapot and looked for tea.

By which you see that we treat Mother as

though she were not one of the cleverest, most practical women in the kingdom.

But she's so very absent-minded in little ways, and as someone said: "She never takes the right turning if she can find the wrong one!"

.   .   .   .

After this I went downstairs and made more tea, which I brought to my own sanctum.

"You can look after yourselves, this morning," I called to the Babes in passing; "I'm going to read Bill's letters in peace.

Then I closed my door.

XXXIII

BEFORE he went Bill said one day:

"When I go to France again what shall I bring you—a little silver rose, or what?"

"Why a little silver rose?" I asked.

"Well, I thought you might like another M.C. And for the second one they give you a bar to the medal. And you wear a little silver rose. It is worn just there!"

He pointed as he spoke, to the centre of the

inch of ribbon on his tunic, then he added meditatively:

"But I don't think we want a silver rose—it would hide the pretty purple stripe! What else would you like instead?"

I smiled at him.

"I'd like *you*. Just bring me back yourself," I said.

And now that he has his "little silver rose" I don't know what to think. I suppose war is too abhorrent to women for them to be able, unreservedly, to appreciate the rewards.

In a prayer lasting all day and every day I give thanks for the glad philosophy which makes my Bill a happy warrior; for the understanding that makes him a kindly one.

That he should be an able warrior doesn't enter into my prayer; yet one pays homage to vitality, and determination.

As for "the little silver rose." Why, how can heroism be sorted out and docketed like that?

The deed for which he won the right to wear it probably was less heroic than some unapparent victory of which he, himself alone, was aware.

But when all is said we shall be human.

I loved my mother's pleasure. We shall love to see the face of Bill's mother when she admires it.

The "pretty purple stripe" will be hidden

after all, but I daresay we shall enjoy the "little silver rose" just as well.

Here is his next letter:

"Darling Aimée,

No letter at all to-day from you!

After writing yesterday I went over and dropped a note for Dick with the news: then, led a patrol and got another Hun!

It was the nicest, most gentlemanly, scrap I have had.

First of all, when coming up from east of —— I spotted a Hun two-seater coming from the lines about 2,000 feet below us. We were at 15,000.

I didn't tackle it well, but the trouble was that none of the others saw it in time. I was afraid to go straight on to it, fearing the observer's gun, and tried to get underneath it.

The Hun fired a signal light as usual, and opened all out and walked away from me. Had the others seen it we could have headed it off.

Bearing in mind the signal light, I turned south again, climbing, and came back to the place about four minutes later.

There, sure enough, were five Hun scouts a thousand feet below us, coming south.

I let four pass and dived on the last one.

Another fellow—Kelly—dived on a second Hun and Scott on a third.

My Hun saw me coming and put his nose down. He caught up with the others by doing this, and then I saw that the leader had turned and was trying to get above me.

I gave up the Hun I had picked out originally and turned on the leader, who was nearly level with me. He swung right across close in front of me, trying to avoid me, and I fired 40 rounds into him. He turned quickly, then went over on his back and fell down all sideways.

I zoomed up hard and found myself level with another, fired at him until he dived off my sights and then turned and found a third an easy mark.

I didn't get very close and my drum ran empty just as he dived away. I probably hit them both, but they were under control.

Kelly and Scott saw no apparent result to their shooting. The Huns just dived away.

As I climbed west to change my drum three more Huns appeared a long way east and well above us, so I decided we had had enough and headed for the lines and home.

This success created more enthusiasm

than any previous one, coming on the announcement of the afternoon.

Kelly and another pilot saw my Hun going down.

Why it was such a nice scrap was that we always remained level with or above the Huns. Not one of them ever got his sights on me to fire, and I'd a Hun to go at every time I looked for one.

.   .   .   .

This morning was dud, so I took a tender and went off to see Dick. I got back at 3.30.

It was awfully nice to see him.

He was with his gun in the battery position, but everything was quiet. I had lunch with him.

His dug-out and gun-emplacement are wonderful—equal for cosiness and cleanliness to a gun turret on a battleship. He says it is becoming quite a show place.

.   .   .   .

No more news and no more bars just now. I am longing for to-morrow to come for your next letter.

I love you, sweetest woman.

All yours,

BILL."

It seems strange that I don't know Bill's brother when they are such rare friends. I wonder if he resents the thought of me? I haven't written to him, but if I do I shall say that if anyone stays at war for two years without a leave they must expect things to happen.

I daresay he is indifferent merely.

XXXIV

AUNT FANNY used to say:

"You'll be sorry for it some day—you mark my words!"

That frightened me very much. I used to brood about it, and "Some day" became mixed up with Hell and the Day of Judgment and Revelations. We lived in Scotland, you see.

This, in a mild form, is one of the "Some days."

I know exactly how Bill felt after writing to tell me of the silver rose. He ached for speech from me, although it couldn't be a reply to his news.

Then next day brought no letter, and the day after that one telling mostly of how little I cared for his article in the Odd Man's magazine.

I know well, too; the chill that comes in the very moment of enthusiasm.

My criticism would have kept until a day when I could kiss him directly afterwards.

"Ma Bien Aimée," he says,

"Your letter of the 7th came to-day. Though I was not displeased with the article myself I felt somehow you wouldn't like it. I still like it, however.

There was no work yesterday, and all night it poured with rain and thundered so hard that we couldn't hear the war.

Up to the present it is very overcast, so I may be able to go to S—— to buy the little silver rose to wear on my ribbon.

The squadron is getting a name, but even we didn't know until last night what a name.

A new pilot arrived and was recognised as a fellow-cadet by R——, who told him he was damned lucky to come to us.

'Oh, yes, I know,' the new man said . . . . 'They told me so at S——. They said it was *the* squadron in France.'

We were frightfully bucked to hear that for what anyone says there is being said throughout the corps in these parts.

The best of it is that we know it's true.

Since the day before the last push we've got down ten Boches certain.

I've been saving up a story to tell you; the wonderful adventure of our crashing 'hun'!

Three mornings ago I took out Faulkner and the 'hun.'

It should have been an offensive patrol of six machines, but the clouds were too low, so I started on a mild and inoffensive line patrol. After half-an-hour of dodging the clouds I gave it up, gave the signal for 'wash-out' and tootled off north alone to have a look at the strafe.

When I got back and landed Faulkner was back, but the 'hun' was still out. About ten minutes later he came in. As he flew over the sheds he was waving frantically. He made a very rocky landing.

His machine was an amazing sight. It was shot and torn to ribbons. We counted fifty-eight holes in it, at least half of them showed that the shots were within a fraction of being vital hits. It was a miracle that the fuselage had not broken in two.

The 'hun' was very excited and it took a long time to understand his story.

When I had signalled 'wash-out' he had turned down the line, seen a balloon away over and decided to strafe it.

He crossed it about five thousand, and when near the balloon saw two enemy two-seaters. He changed his mind and attacked them. One he hit and crashed. Then from above came four red scouts and from below 'Archie.' For ten minutes, while he struggled to get back to the lines, losing height fast all the way, the Huns dived at him and fired at him.

He felt his elevator go slack suddenly, and looking round saw that the control on one side had been shot away. The whole machine seemed to go sloppy and groggy. A shot hit one cylinder and his engine began to miss.

Finally as they neared the lines, when a Hun dived at him, he stalled and turned and the Hun overshot him. He fired then and raked the Hun up and down the fuselage, and he went down almost promptly and crashed. They were now only about 200 feet off the ground.

At last our 'hun' crossed the trenches, being fired at by the Boches and cheered by our Tommies as he crawled over.

He came home flying low all the way. His machine was a 'write-off.' There was hardly a part of it untouched.

As his temporary flight commander I strafed him violently for playing the fool, and told him his luck was more than he deserved. But to myself I acknowledged that it was awfully plucky to struggle on as he did. It was his fifth trip over the line and his first scrap—though he had seen one other.

He will not attempt to repeat the performance. When his excitement wore off he had a big re-action, and he realizes now what inexperience may do. We have great hopes for him as he gets his balance.

Well, that's all the news—except that you may not have heard that I love you.

All yours, every moment.

BILL."

For one thing I am thankful, and it is that Bill is able to remain cold in moments of greatest turmoil. I have this comfort, that though he will shirk nothing through fear, he will allow reason to be his guide.

XXXV

AT last he has had the sort of letter—the only sort of letter—a man should receive from his wife.

"Oh, my dear," he answers,

"When you write as you do to-day, when you tell me of your longings and your thoughts, I can hardly bear to stay here.

For I want you too, my wonderful lover; and just to want you so intensely and to know you want me is exquisite happiness.

You make all my life so complete.

I am sitting in my hut now clad in a shirt and shorts—my Suvla ones. I have been having a cold bath after a very hot game of tennis, and feel beautifully cool.

Before lunch I led an offensive patrol. There was not much excitement; one Hun two-seater got in our way and only just managed to escape. I dived on him but could not get very near, and though I fired 50 rounds he continued to dive, straight down—we were looking into the streets of ——, and at 8,000 feet I gave it up, as that was too low to be safe so far over the lines.

I spent half-an-hour alone after the patrol trying to persuade another two-seater further north to come over our side of the lines and be shot down, but like all these German people he was very unreasonable and seemed to prefer that I should do it over the Rhine. I didn't follow him quite so far, however.

I dined last night with —— Squadron

at their farewell dinner. They are moving to another aerodrome.

I got lots of congratulations, and it was rather quaint to be talking 'shop' on equal terms with men whom in England we heard of as among the best fighting scout experts.

After dinner I risked what is now my wife's money to the extent of 10 francs at roulette. At any rate I borrowed 10 francs to start playing, as I had none in my pockets: and promptly paid that back and finished 12 francs up.

My luck is always in!

Last night—earlier—did a line patrol on which nothing occurred.

During the patrol, while I was at 12,000 feet, I spotted Dick's battery by a gun flash.

When I was there the previous day the major had challenged me to find it from the air because he said they had been in the same place for weeks and the Boche hadn't spotted them yet.

Of course I had the advantage of having been there on the ground. When I looked for it I simply followed with my eye the route I had taken—and just at the moment my eye stopped at the exact spot there was a flash from the gun itself!

Afterwards I went down low over the

position, 'chucked' a few stunts and waved to Dick.

.   .   .   .

Mother's letter is quaint. But they worry a great deal too much. You will do them a lot of good when you go.

Just going to tea now. I send you all my love.

BILL.

P.S.—To-day, by the way, your letters were of the 6th and the 8th. One of the 7th came yesterday and one of the 5th two days earlier. The 6th has been hung up somewhere.

I'm feeling awfully pleased with things to-day because you got my news this morning—Tuesday."

.   .   .   .

I have no time to think.

On Monday the Babes go again to school, and it is staggering to discover that nearly every garment worn by either needs buttons or hooks or darns.

As well as that they must be fed three times every day.

A woman with children to care for might just as well resign herself to the fact that to them

must be devoted every single moment of her
waking time.

Someone has to do it. Plainly I see that.
Every second spent at this table means neglect
of a necessary trifle.

I shall miss them when they go, yet I shall
breathe once more—and I won't cook at all!

But even now I refuse to scurry over Bill's
letters; so, having seen the Babes begin their
porridge—Bey eats hers willingly because a
Mr. Quimper lives at the bottom of the bowl
and waits for her to say good-morning—I
carried my tray up here to my sanctum.

"Aimée, dearest one," he begins,

"Your words were so wonderful again
when I read them to-day in your letter of
Saturday.

Just as dreadfully as you I am longing
also. But we have not too long to wait.

Things are very quiet again and I am
getting only one job a day.

I was to have done an O.P. at 6 this
morning, but when I got up at 5 a.m. it
was so cloudy that I changed it to a line
patrol and took only two others.

It was difficult to see, and we came
back after 40 minutes.

Since then I have slept most of the day,
as it is too hot to do anything else.

I don't think I've any news and very little to talk about.

All my love, sweetest lover.

BILL."

Foolish one, it is your handwriting, and your words of love, I cherish. What is "news" to me? I can read the morning paper for that, can't I?

XXXVI

THE church bells ring—but I sit here wrapped in an overall. Betty is covering the kitchen table with "ingredients." We are to make a cake for school.

But I must read first what my Bill says and then all the while we stir flour and eggs and chocolate flavouring and things I can be thinking of his words.

"My own wife,

There was no letter from you to-day. The post is very stupid. I love so much to talk to you and hear you talk to me *every* day.

This morning I did a line patrol, as it

was too misty again for an O.P. There was also a westerly gale blowing and at 17,000 feet we could hardly move—in fact, we lost ground and were blown over the lines unless we put our noses down and did 100 miles an hour against it. We saw nothing all the time.

I went to the range yesterday, and won 10 francs from the brigade machine-gun officer.

I told you, I think, that he has a competition in which we pay him one franc for every drum we fire at the target unless we score five per cent. or more—in which case he pays one franc per cent. I fired 130 rounds and got 13 hits in seven dives—or 10 per cent.

The weather is intensely hot again, and I shall sleep this afternoon.

There may be an O.P. to lead this evening, but no orders are through yet.

The new flight commander is due here to-morrow, so I shall relinquish command of the flight again then. He is a good man.

He was here when I first came, and went home sick about a month ago.

The O.C. is still in England and is due back next week. He knows nothing of our success since he went. He will be fearfully excited when he comes back.

Last night I lay awake for a long time just thinking and longing.

My dear one! All yours.

BILL."

Oh, I wish we—whatever it is that makes us, it is not our bodies—could go out consciously and meet in the night time. I, too, lie awake—thinking of him. Why can we not know it at the time? What is this barrier and why can't we triumph over it?

XXXVII

"MOST precious One.

I've been waiting so impatiently for your letter acknowledging my news.

It came to-day, and I am more thrilled than when I heard about the bar. It is lovely, isn't it, to have our sympathies so intensely, so vitally mutual? I live only for you, dearest lover, and when you are happy I am thrilled to ecstasy.

It turned out as I expected.

Your mother heard the news before

leaving. My people have not written about it yet.

.   .   .   .

This morning I led an O.P. It was quite an amusing one, for right at the start one impudent Hun sailed over our heads while we were climbing—*on our side* of the lines.

We were at about 9,000 and he was at 14,000 or 15,000 feet. He just ignored us, and though I climbed all out I couldn't reach him. Ultimately we lost him.

When we crossed at 14,000 I chased two Huns off the lines and then turned southeast. Two more Huns appeared below—one a bit east and the other further south.

I made a feint of going for the south one while closing up gradually on the other; then turned suddenly and dived on him.

He dived too, and I never got nearer than 100 yards. We dived—the Hun and the whole of our patrol—from 16,000 to 9,000 feet, and I fired 45 rounds and another fellow fired 30 rounds. The Hun went on diving, however, and ultimately went out of sight.

When I turned and climbed I looked down, as I thought into the streets of ——. But after ten minutes hard flying against the slight wind I looked down again and I was still over the streets of ——.

We had been over the other side of another town miles further east.

I saw two more Huns a long way over, but they simply would not come and give us a chance at them.

The weather is still intensely hot. Yesterday afternoon I played tennis in pyjamas, and after perspiring beautifully had a cold bath in my hut. This afternoon I have only just energy left to lie down and sleep until tea time.

Do you know that I love you? Darling Aimée, I want you and soon....

All yours,

BILL."

Oh, I wonder how soon he means when he says "soon"?

I want to know and I'm frightened to know. I want to be able to count the days, and yet I think I shall be worn to a shadow if I do—and what joy would a shadow be to Bill?

We want each other to kiss and love, and we want to see each other.

It's very difficult to explain why spiritual union is not enough, any more than mere bodily union would be enough. I suppose it's because—on this earth anyway—we are human; and because there must be something beyond—above!

When Bill comes back to me I think I will weep. Tears come to my eyes even at the thought.

XXXVIII

WE are in the train at last.

At 6.30 this morning the seventh or ninth wonder dragged me from sleep. Hers was the ruthless knocking of one who has to rise right out of her dreams and take hold of a scrubbing brush.

A moment later Betty ran into my room.

"I don't know which'll be the nicest of all the journey, darling," she sighed with flushed cheeks.

I clung to my pillow.

"Nicest?" I cried—then I realized that at seven and a half you appreciate trains and railway stations even if you have to start in the dead of night with the promise of a broiling day.

She sits now at the opposite end of the compartment,—which our gods have given us all to ourselves,—and looks a picture of cool enjoyment. I suppose you may when your skirts finish just below your waist and your socks just above your ankles!

She is nursing her "baby" and explaining in an undertone that we are moving and not the fields and trees and sky.

Bey is devouring a sequel to "Daddy-long-legs."

And at last I may read Bill's letter.

Every moment has led up to this one. The thrill of breaking the envelope never grows less. It is the summit of my day.

"Dear, dear woman," he says,
"I got the finished copy of your big photograph this morning.

I don't know why you are always on the verge of being apologetic about it, and I don't quite know why other people are not satisfied with it. I love it.

But after all it is only a photograph, and whatever it is that is lacking in this one is lacking more or less in every photograph.

I'm sure my last one, with which I'm quite satisfied, conveys nothing more to anybody than a flat reproduction of the shape of my features.

I love your photograph. I love it, just because it helps me to visualise you physically; and when I can do that it is much easier to picture your more abstract

attributes—your sweetness, your comprehension, your passion. Oh, you dear pagan!

.   .   .   .

I am sitting under an open marquee, on
a huge double deck-chair made by the
Odd Man, listening to ragtime on the
gramaphone. It is burning hot and I am
wearing just a shirt, cotton breeches and
socks and slippers.

I haven't flipped yet to-day; I expect a
patrol at 7.30 this evening when all the
Huns will be up.

The Odd Man's big deck-chair is quite
wonderful. It will seat ten. It is made of
rough timber and cocoanut matting.

.   .   .   .

Talking of ragtime! Did you ever see
my ragtime words written to the ragtime
music composed by Martin under the
influence of Heidseick? I wish he were
here?

But that is not my greatest wish in the
world!

I got a quaint combined letter from
home to-day about the bar.

Mother is pleased. She hardly dare say
how much—but she pleads with me not to
try to get any more decorations!

She said exactly the same thing over the first award.

. . . .

Last evening after dinner, before a large audience, the Odd Man and I had a topping discussion on the war, the peace, Germany's future position and our attitude to her, the Russian revolution, and then later, conscientious objections, industrial unrest and Socialism and Christianity.

If it had been an argument, or a debate, I would have claimed a complete decision on all points. But it wasn't. It was a discussion, and was therefore so much more satisfactory.

It was really good. I wish I could reproduce it, but I can't.

Do you remember that when you said you'd like to meet the Odd Man I wondered and doubted whether you would, because apart from his good-nature and sincerity and quick repartee he had little to appeal to you—having the stereotyped 'country gentleman' attitude of his type toward political and sociological things? However, I do think he tries to get outside these traditional prejudices—and it must be difficult.

. . . .

Your letter of Wednesday last arrived

to-day also and made me all happy all over—all over again.

Bien Aimée, it is so wonderful to possess you, to have such a dear, dear wife. It is becoming almost too much now that I can count the days until I see you.

Darlingest, I want you unspeakably.

All, all yours,

BILL."

.   .   .   .

Now we are in the second train and soon we shall reach our station.

Having decided upon the one way to fill in the hour's wait we commandeered a corner table in a refreshment room, which would have been intolerable on a cold or rainy day, but, to-day was preferable to the suffocating blaze of sunshine outside. Betty ate four bath buns. Bey discovered cracknell biscuits and rejoiced. With them she drank lemonade and needed it, I'm sure! But Betty sighed for tea. So did I, and we had a large pot full.

.   .   .   .

Their delight at the thought of meeting everyone, from the "Head" downward, makes me realize gladly how the methods at this school must contrast with the rigid, stupid discipline of the place to which I used, loathingly, to return each term.

"We've loved being with you, darling," Betty has just announced.

"Yes, we have," seconded the smaller Babe. Betty proceeded:

"But of course if you've *got* to do lessons you might just as well fire away—otherwise you'd find yourself in the same class as infants like Bey!"

This couldn't pass, of course. The protest came at once. "I'm not an infant—I'm seven and a half!" Bey shouted.

Betty looked all her condescension as she glanced downward from her height.

"Well, what's that?" she queried. "Wait until you're *my* age and you'll see!"

What Bey had to wait for wasn't explained, but I hope—though long after she has passed Betty's milestone—a husband as delicious as Bill!

XXXIX

THE Babes are delivered safely!

That sounds as though someone had had twins, but it means only that Betty and Bey have returned to school.

I shouldn't care to have been one of the staff

when the whole concern moved from the coast to the country, but I should imagine that now they feel relieved.

Stoics perhaps, but not ordinary mortals, could preserve calm of mind in the throes of raids by air, and bombardment by sea, while responsible for fifty children belonging to nearly as many sets of parents.

.   .   .   .

For forty-eight hours I haven't heard Bill speak—or *seen* him speak, I should say, perhaps.

A while longer on this journey and half-an-hour in Barnes' old crock of a taxi that feeds now-a-days on a mixed diet and resents it rowdily, then the seventh or ninth wonder will appear carrying a bundle of letters—two at least from France.

It is so lovely to have a husband—not any old husband—but my husband!

.   .   .   .

There are three!

Two were written on one day, and each is very short.

"Dearest one," says the first,
    "A line in case I don't catch the post with a longer letter to-night.

Am just off to —— to get my hair cut and shall be back, I hope, in time to write.

Out on patrol this morning I was hit on the forehead by 'Archie.' My goggles, which I had pushed back, were smashed, but saved my head.

I love you.

BILL."

Well, "that's *that*," as Bill would say! I am obliged to sit here and read that my whole world has been hit on the head by a piece of shell; that he was saved by the merest chance!

I can just manage to remind myself that all life is "chance"—and so keep calm. What else can I do?

The second letter was written during the afternoon.

"Dearest,

I have just got back to find your letter of the 14th waiting for me. We had a nice lunch at —— and bought lots of things like pyjamas and underlinen and pictures and toilet creams.

Just in time for the post. I still love you.
BILL."

The third one, posted next day, contains the news I have waited for and longed to hear.

"My Wife,

I know you'd be disappointed at the scrappiness of my letters yesterday, but I hadn't time to write more.

Things are still very quiet—partly because the weather is so unsettled. It is raining and thundering again now.

After lunch I went to the range and fired a drum and then went for lunch with —— Squadron.

Holt was there too, and when we came away we got up to 2,000 together and at my signal we 'rolled', at the same moment. This we did four times, keeping quite near each other all the time. Then we spun and did Immelmann's and finally dived together at the sheds.

When we got over our own aerodrome we did the same performance equally successfully.

.   .   .   .

The time gets nearer for my leave.

Two fellows went yesterday and I am one of the next two.

We shall leave, if present arrangements continue, a few days after their return.

Where do you wish to meet me?

At Folkestone or in London? I rather think the latter.

I got your letter of Saturday when I got back.

I loved to read of you making the blue crêpe-de-chine things because they are for me.

All, all yours.

BILL.

P.S.—I'd nearly forgotten the news. Grahaeme has been awarded the M.C. As I told you before, he is my right hand man. He always flies close behind me, and I always know he will be there.

I had a little bit of M.C. ribbon all made up ready, and when the wire came through last evening I was able to fish it out of my pocket promptly, and pin it on to his tunic.

. . . .

Do you love me?
I worship you.

BILL."

XL

OLD Witchell came this morning to pick fruit to send to Molly. When I heard the bell I hung out of my bedroom window.

"Hullo!" I called.

He looked up—his round face beaming.

"Good-marnin'!" he called. "I was just a-wondrin' if you was a-comin' t'help me gather them chirries!"

I laughed at him. He makes you laugh.

"I'm not dressed," I answered, leaning on the ledge to indicate that I didn't intend to dress either.

"Well you do the lazy this marnin'!" he exclaimed.

"Oh, no, I'm not," I contradicted. "I've been very busy—I've been writing my letter to my husband."

With a doubtful expression he scratched his head.

"Well, I do be wondrin' what you have t'say t'one another *ivry* day!" he cried, and added, "How do he be?—Gettin' on nicely?"

"Splendidly, thanks. And how are Jack and Jim?"

"Fine, thank 'ee. Jack he be back we' his ship be now. He were a bit quiet like. Not the same lad his mother tould him."

"What did he say to that?"

"He didn't say nothin'. But I reckon he do have seen things t'make a lad quiet. And when do 'ee be expectin' 'eer husband home—have 'ee any idea?"

I drew a deep breath. It had to be said

sometime—the thing I dared not say even to myself.

I looked across at the sky where it meets the ridge of the Downs.

"Oh, make it true," I prayed, and aloud I answered:

"A fortnight to-day he hopes to be in England!"

And when the words had passed my lips I breathed again.

My fear left me.

He will come, I know.

.   .   .   .

Old Witchell's voice brought me to myself.

"Be-ant 'ee lonely all be 'eerself in this big house?"

Truly I believe that if I had explained to him that I am not alone—that Bill is with me all the while—he would have understood.

But I couldn't call it out of the bedroom window, so I just said: "No—I'm hardly ever lonely!"

"'Taint reet for no one," he replied, seriously. Then he brightened up.

"I tell 'ee what—'ee come along this after-noon an' have a cup a tea wi' me and the Missus. She'll be reet glad!" he said.

.   .   .   .

Bill's letter was lying on the table. I took it up to read again:—

"Darlingest,

Because there were two editions of the mail yesterday I got no letter to-day. Car même, I can read your other one again. We are all just setting out by tender for a Canadian camp, where a big base-ball game is taking place. Grahaeme of M.C. and blasphemy fame is in charge of the outing.

This morning I led the early patrol. It was a perfect morning and we went a long way over at 16,000, but saw nothing.

I have been trying to make everybody in the flight roll, and two of them do it now. So when the patrol was nearly over I gave a signal and rolled—Grahaeme promptly did the same and Holt also;— and we came back over the lines in a big 'V,' throwing ourselves all over the sky. Once I turned over on my back and flew like that for half a minute.

. . . . .

After breakfast I went to do the climbing test and stunting I told you of, before the H.Q. Staff. It was quite unexciting. I just did everything I could think of and then came home.

The Odd Man left to-day for England.

He said he would try to look you up. I hope he does.

Do you know how I love you? I cannot calculate it. My lovely lover.

BILL."

XLI

SOMEONE has written an article "On leave."

It is the outburst of a soldier who goes back to a pleasant calm country and hears his own people "*talk* war."

They ask him questions and he answers vaguely, for he knows that if he were to speak his bitterness as bitterly as he feels it they, though kind and forbearing, without comprehending in the least would think him a little mad.

He sneers.

"What do they know of this Hell of war?"

How *can* they know? With the most vivid imagination how can they know?

But, on the other hand, what does he know of the Hell of those who stay at home?

What of all the fathers who, willingly, would

give their lives for their sons; and the mothers
whose soldier boys are their babies; and the
wives who wait and fear and ache for them.

There are two sides to this, soldier!

Who is to say which suffers more—and who
is to know?

.   .   .   .

"Aimée, dear one," my lover says to-day.

"The letter I received from you this
morning—written on your railway
journey—was just lovely.

By now I suppose you are back again.
I hope your mother will have returned
with you.

Have you noticed—of course you
have—that my letters get much briefer
lately? I find much less to write about
than formerly. The new impressions seem
to be pretty well exhausted—and besides
that we do so little lately that there's not a
lot of news for you.

But I'm waiting to hear something of
your short stories. What about them?

In the latest official communiqué
appears the following: 'Hostile Aircraft.
—In the evening Lieut. B—— (your
husband) while on offensive patrol drove
down a German machine out of control.
He then attacked a second, which was

driven down and crashed. Lieut. G—— of the same Squadron drove down a hostile scout out of control.'

Bloodthirsty!

But I love you, dear lover.

All, all yours.

BILL."

XLII

I DON'T know how other wives feel when their husbands are due for leave.

Nothing so wonderful ever has happened to me before.

Our marriage was an adventure—and I love adventure! It promised a lot of things—companionship, interest, someone on whom to concentrate affection, and from whom affection would be given.

It promised much, but not this ecstasy that is so calm, so radiant.

It envelops me. I am possessed by a miracle of—what is it?

I think it must be *love*!

.   .   .   .

Bill becomes less articulate as the time of our meeting draws closer. And in my letters to him I am more garrulous, I notice. I tell him silly details—about my new frock and hat, and the shoes which Monsieur, who makes for queens and kings, won't promise to deliver until the very last moment, although they were ordered a month ago and he charges the earth! His expression suggests, "Take it or leave it." So, of course, you just take it, and leave it at that.

If they don't fit, goodness knows what I'll do, for my others are in rags.

Then I tell him about the new crêpe-de-chine "undies," and the new "boudoir" caps, and the absurd little jacket to go with them—to wear when we sit up in bed with our heads close together, drinking our morning tea.

It isn't the slightest use anyone complaining that these details are superfluous in war time. They are more necessary than ever they were to the man *who has lived war* for months.

"My dear, dear Wife," he says.

"I got your letter of Thursday the 19th today. I love it. I liked the bits about your clothes and things.

You want to know how I am. Awfully fit except for a touch of that Suvla indigestion during the last week.

And now! What are your plans for when I get to England?

Where will you meet me and where shall we stay?

Faulkner left to-day on his leave, and if the other fellows return to time I may leave here on the 3rd or 4th and get to London the following day. That is a week next Wednesday or Thursday or Friday. Of course when I know definitely I will wire you.

I got the enclosed letter to-day from Dick. I hope to see him again before I come on leave.

Darling lover, I want you more than I dare realise. Do you love me? All my love.

BILL."

XLIII

How am I to exist until he comes?

On Sunday, as we sat round the tea table in her tiny parlour crammed with coloured glass ornaments—"presents from somewhere"—and crinkled paper and enlargements of photographs, Mrs. Witchell said:

"I don't hold wi' flyin' .... The Lord He

di'n' give us no wings.... 'Tain't proper....
'Tis callin' forth His mispleasure 'tis!"

"The Lord didn't give us fins—and yet Jack
sails on the sea!" I reminded her maliciously,
because the little arrow of foreboding cut
through my heart and, as she had sent it,
humanly I wanted her to share the pain.

I went on chewing at the large chunk of
home-made cake and watched her expression
grow puzzled, then uneasy: but soon it became
placid again.

"'Tis diff'rent.... 'Tain't the same," she
said—and that was enough.

As she seemed to know so much of what the
Lord thinks, I wanted to ask her if He approved
of war; of the big shells from the big guns with
which Jack and Jim are obliged to massacre
their kind; of all this perversion of reason; of
the useless, silly waste of it all.

But instead I went on eating cake.

Old Witchell, in his pale blue shirt sleeves,
best satin spotted tie, and best black trousers
and waistcoat, sat on my other side.

Jerry and Gwendolen-Ivy, solidly munching,
stared, goggle-eyed, at whoever spoke. Mary's
baby lay on the horsehair sofa, with Mary—so
motherly glad—on the edge to keep it from
rolling off. And every time Witchell turned his
beaming scarlet face toward her the baby
yelled.

"Yew fill his lil' belly too full—that what I says!" he cried at last in exasperation.

"That I don't," denied Mary, with a toss of her head. "'Tis a princess could be no better looked to than my babe.... 'Tis yew wi' your great voice a'-shoutin' at the lamb like what you did that day!"

Into her arms she gathered the small bundle.

"There now," she crooned. "His Dad be a'-comin' soon he be..... Never 'ee take no heed then.... His Dad what never see his lil' face—he be a'-comin' soon—soon!"

And as I heard the poetry of her voice I knew herself was with the sailor who since three weeks before their babe was born hasn't seen his wife.

Jack's best friend is Mary's man. The two work together on the big ship somewhere on the wide sea—when you pass your days encircled by the ridge of the Downs, all beyond also seems beyond measurement, you know—and as Jack is one of those who live in other's joy you can imagine how the father is allowed to pivot every conversation round one subject—Mary and the babe—the babe and Mary!

.   .   .   .

Oh, I wish I could lose consciousness until he comes—or wish he could be kept in a glass-case until the day.

"My dear one," he says.

"I'm out on the advanced landing ground again. It is rather a dud day and so far we have had nothing to do. This morning I was up at three o'clock as I had to lead at O.P as soon as it was light, but the clouds were too low, so I went to bed again at 5 a.m.

I had no success yesterday. When I got to where Dick had been I found that they had moved away. I had tea with the C.R.E. and whole bundles of Brigadiers and red tabs again, and I got home at 9 a.m. There was a lovely letter from you waiting for me.

I am just going to fly back to the aerodrome for the mail. It is Friday now and by next Wednesday—just imagine! I can't. Can you hear me shouting for my machine, and can you see the mechanics running out.

Later.

The Aerodrome.
I landed here ten minutes ago and found the most lovely letter of all—the one written on Monday telling me delicious things. Dear, dear Aimée, my ecstasy is almost too much.

All, all yours.

BILL."

XLIV

TO-DAY I came home.

Suddenly I couldn't bear the solitude. Although it is Sunday and I had arranged to come here on Monday or Tuesday I just couldn't wait. The noise and wracket are welcome. The restlessness matches my mood. Mother understands. She wasn't a bit surprised to see me.

I can't sleep. I don't want to. I want to talk about Bill.

Mother listened until her eyes, which are most alert at midnight, began to close, and now I am reading his last letter again.

"You darling," he says:

"You thrill me too much. A lovelier letter than yesterday's came for me to-day and made me faint with delight. My dear, dear woman, I love you—your mind and your body—beyond all expression.

The letter from you was written on the 26th in bed and on the day when you got no letter from me.

And now, the news. I've got a flight;

and in about three weeks I expect to be gazetted Captain and Flight-Commander.

It isn't 'B' Flight; that is my only regret. I so much wanted 'B' Flight, and all the fellows in it and the personnel wanted me to have it too.

You see since Romney left the Squadron I have been running 'B' Flight with the exception of a few days.

More news. Kyrle has been awarded an M.C.

The wire came last night. We are all glad. He is, as I have often told you, a wonderful pilot and a topping patrol leader, with lots of strafe and lots of caution.

Still more news. The wing adjutant rang up this afternoon to say that my leave will start on Wednesday or Thursday; more probably Wednesday.

If I fly over I ought to be in London the same evening; if not, about mid-day the following day.

I must catch the post with this, as it may be the last letter you can receive before I arrive. But I will go on writing until I leave here, of course.

Do you love me? 'Yes, Bill.'

BILL."

XLV

WE had had lunch and were drinking coffee.

Purcell entered with a telegram, which she handed to me.

I tore it open and read:

"Leave commenced sooner than expected. Arriving Victoria 2 p.m. to-day. Meet me Savoy Hotel."

I looked at mother and Maisie, who were staring. Then I looked at the clock. The small hand said "two," and the large hand almost covered it. I sprang from my chair.

"Mother!" I cried. "Bill's train will be in the station *now*!... Oh, what shall I do?"

.   .   .   .

Mother and Maisie and Purcell helped me into a frock. The new hat had come and proved to be one of those perfect affairs that adapt themselves to an emergency; the shoes we had wrenched from Monsieur earlier in the day; and when the long chain of turquoise matrix had been clasped, and the last whisper of powder had been whisked on, to what Maisie calls "the flaps" of my nose, I kissed them all and flew down to the waiting taxi.

.   .   .   .

At the Savoy, dozens of soldier men—lots of them with Flying Corps caps—drifted in and out. I sat in a corner from where I best could see, and my heart did all sorts of silly things.

Though most men may not be as wonderful as Bill, their uniforms are not unlike.

.   .   .   .

The twisting doorway turned again. I saw him.

There was no mistaking when he came at length.

Straight to the desk he went—for we had arranged that I should take a room, though not so soon.

I saw him speak, and after a pause, during which the official consulted a book, I saw him receive an answer, then slowly turn away; and I knew that, immediately, he would telephone to ask my whereabouts.

I knew, too, that he would go to me at once.

Then I stopped being another person. I knew that it was necessary to move.

Next moment I had touched his arm.

"Bill!" I said.

He turned to look at me.

He seemed to look and look—and then he spoke.

"Aimée!" he whispered.

And I knew the word meant "Beloved."

PART II

I

To-DAY Bill goes to France again. A moment ago we stood outside the aerodrome, and all about us the fields shone in an amazing splendour. Beyond these fields was the sea.

Overhead, like black or silver streaks against the blue heaven, aeroplanes darted about. Engines buzzed and droned; shots followed one another in staccato succession; a machine rose vertically from the target, to whirl and dive again.

I felt Bill's excitement—his eagerness once more to handle the mechanism, to return to the work into which he throws every ounce of his capacity; to the men in whose skill he delights with almost an artistic appreciation.

His eyes followed a little speck on the horizon.

"Oh, you would love it.... How I just long to take you, too," he cried.

Quickly my gaze came back to his face, for he had voiced my most ardent wish.

"That would be wonderful," I said. Then, so that he should know I didn't grieve and how glad I felt in the sunshine, I added: "But I'm happy.... I'm perfectly content that you should go." And as his clasp tightened on my hand I smiled, for my joyousness surely must mean all would be well—that he and I were parting only for a little while!

But I wanted an assurance from his lips, and my eyes looked into his to see the truth for fear he should utter words merely for my peace of heart.

"You are coming back?... You *know* you're coming back?" I questioned.

Seriously he turned to me and spoke with absolute conviction. "I'm certain—quite certain," he said.

After that no cloud remained.

.   .   .   .

For an hour we had motored through lanes and villages—and now the man at the wheel is taking me on alone.

It's funny how glad I feel.

II

In the train there were two very small boys.

They wore pink and white striped blouses and minute pink linen trousers, fastening on the shoulders with straps.

They had corn-coloured mops of hair, blue

eyes, and impossibly perfect complexions. The mother, a woman who looked as though she had no thought to spare for herself, wiped her face with a handkerchief.

"They've been travelling for hours," she said. "They are just about fed up!"

Then, while the younger one clambered on to my knee to tug at the chain round my neck, she went on to explain that they were going North to a grandmother to escape the bombs which had fallen several times about their part of the world.

"That one—his nerves is awful!... But don't let him worry you like that," she pleaded, bending forward to try to lift him away.

Puckering up his face he clung to the chain; and at this the other one, realizing that he missed an excitement, stretched across until I had to clutch him also to prevent a fall.

The mother sighed. Her expression suggested that the gods were using their last straw.

"Why not leave them to me and go to sleep?" I said; and then after that, while they turned me into a game quite ruthlessly, I reflected on grandmothers and mothers and how they come to pass.

It was when we changed, however, that I longed for Bill to see us.

"My porter will bring your luggage,"...

I assured the mother.... "Don't bother about it at all."

But when I saw that no words would persuade her to leave it, I said I would be responsible for the live stock, and to this she agreed, but on the platform they seemed to become shorter and fatter, until they looked like round fluffy balls.

One on either hand they toddled placidly until one of them without warning yelled:

"Mummy!... Mummy!... Where Mummy?"

Fearfully I looked back, to see his mummy in the throes of suitcases and a perambulator, so, stooping down, I gathered this infant into one arm, without daring to leave hold of his brother.

"Mummy's coming soon," ...I whispered .... "Be a good boy and I'll give you lots of nice things."

Whether or no he heard didn't matter, for he rediscovered the chain about my neck, and with little grunts and babbles of delight began to tug at it for all he was worth.

A very immaculate elderly man stepped aside from the door of the compartment and frigidly helped us in.

Then after staring with disapproval and perplexity for some moments he made up his mind to speak.

"Your husband at the war, my dear?" he asked.

Panicked at the thought of the damage they might do themselves, I clung to the struggling infants, clutching both in one bundle on my knee.

"Yes!... He's an airman," I gasped.

Over his eyeglass he drew his brows together.

"Dear me... Dear me!" he muttered—and I knew he was pitying Bill.

.   .   .   .

This "Hydro" is a terrible place. At dinner I felt uncharitable and my own distaste annoyed me, for I would like to feel well disposed toward all people.

I left before the meal was half way over and came to this corner of the lounge to write to Bill.

To look at some of the people here is to dread age; but I know that in the course of things we must grow old some day; and when that happens to me I want to be like the woman who has tucked herself into the corner opposite.

She is wearing a frock that hangs in folds and draperies, and her white hair is piled up on her head with a jewelled comb.

She puffs away at a cigarette in a long slim holder; and glances humorously at me.

She loves and respects her age, and she means everyone else to love and respect it too.

To-morrow Joan should come. I am longing for her; but even more I long for my first letter from Bill.

Now I will go to bed and morning will not seem so remote.

III

IT has come—my letter!

"Darling," it says,

"Gazetted to-day! Am just leaving on one of the newest type of scout machine.

All my love.

BILL."

I might have been certain he would find a moment to write and send me all his love!

Again I feel as I felt after our last parting that I am not alone. Even in this strange place Bill's thoughts are with me.

Wasn't I cross last night?

It was disgusting of me.

Indeed it is a pity that I, who have so much, should fail to understand that all men and women are the result of circumstance and that to criticize is to prove my limitation.

I wonder if Bill's waking thought was of me? But of course it was, for I am with him all the while.

Now I will get up and go to meet Joan.

It was a splendid idea for us to spend her holiday together. I expect we shall talk of Bill most of the time.

.   .   .   .

Joan is very content to sit on the verandah, or to walk without an aim, listening to the tales Bill has told me, and to the account of his leave, for she saw him only during the three or four days at home.

She is most thrilled to hear of the evening in town with Romney and Faulkener and Grahaeme and the others. She wishes she had been with us and I wish it too, though I was selfish and wanted Bill all to myself.

Next time he comes on leave we must persuade her to go to town with us and give her a riotous time.

Anyway she must be with us in Paris afterwards. She has too many of Bill's possibilities to be allowed to waste herself in one groove.

I have told her also of the five perfect days on the golf course by the sea; and of Bill's pleasure in my "style," though I played so atrociously, and of his lecture on concentration because I became absorbed in an account of our opponent's hospital work instead of thinking of my next shot.

She laughed much about the little man who, in spite of the fact that bombs fall regularly in the street where he has his office, has tempted providence by supplying himself with socks enough to last for many years—because wool is going to be so scarce and expensive after the war!

.   .   .   .

Each day brings nearer the first letter from France.

To-morrow it should come.

The days seem unreal and so do the people here—except Joan, who is of the same flesh and blood as Bill.

Last night there was a dance. The music got into my veins and I longed for my lover to come.

He didn't though—and so I enticed Joan into the corridor and bullied her into learning a fox-trot and a one-step and a hesitation waltz. To-night someone concocted a concert in aid of the military hospital. The whole thing seemed to be like a caricature. Very fat men and very thin women—or very thin men and very fat women—all crusted and rusted into grooves, sat and listened while performers from among them did their turns.

The few young ones seemed all pose and meaningless sagacity. Uncomfortably I wondered what ailed my point of view, and was relieved to find that Joan wanted to leave the place.

"Let's go to bed," she whispered, and as we passed the alcove I saw the woman whose growing old has been accomplished with grace.

She lay among her cushions, knitting leisurely—her long cigarette holder gripped between her teeth.

Both the holder and the teeth probably were expensive, but it is not her bank balance that gives her distinction, for all the others look full of cheque-books.

Just a tiny glint of irony tinged the tolerant amusement of her glance.

She is very wise, I think.

I want Bill.

I feel all incomplete.

IV

THE letter has come at last.

It seems ages since I heard from my love, but really it is four days only.

Now something should arrive from him each morning and the days will be worthy of the sunshine once more.

"Darling," he says,

"I got back to the squadron half-an-hour ago—too late for the post. I find lots of things have been happening—but I must tell you first of my crossing.

It wasn't at all nice really. I'd never seen a —— scout before, nor the type of engine used in it, but when they asked me if I could fly one I said 'yes' promptly.

I think it would have been all right if everything had been normal, but the petrol and air adjustment was frightfully difficult to work. A fitter spent half-an-hour trying to get the engine started and to keep it going and to show me how to do it, and then I spent twenty minutes trying to taxi out across the aerodrome.

Finally I got desperate and the next time the engine started—about the eighth—I opened all out and went right off.

After you had left me I watched the taxi disappearing down the lane and wondered what were your thoughts.

I met a fellow I knew and talked with him for an hour, and then about 11.30 I was told there would be a —— scout for

me, so I went down to the mess and wrote
a note to you before I left.

Getting away was an awful business. I
had to pack my haversack in no space at
all, and as I had to wear a big life-belt—
in case I landed in the water—I was
horribly cramped and felt sure I'd never
be able to fly a strange machine like that.

When I did get off I hardly knew it. I
was barely breathing for wondering if the
engine would stop for the ninth time when
I crawled over the sheds. The engine
wasn't going all out but just enough to lift
me from the ground.

However, it improved after I got
clear of the aerodrome, and I climbed
up to 5,000 feet before it gave me any
trouble.

Then it started dropping its revolutions
and, when I tried to re-adjust it, stopped
altogether.

I got it started again when I had fallen
to 1,500 feet, and without further trouble
climbed to 7,000 feet and headed out to sea.

Then it gave out again and I had to turn
back.

I felt horribly wild with it now, so
when, after losing 2,000 feet, I got it
again, I headed straight across for the
French coast, which I could see.

I can't describe to you the tenseness with which I watched my engine for the next twenty minutes. Every two or three minutes it started to fail, slightly, and I had to work cautiously at the hand pump to keep up pressure in the petrol tank, and very gingerly to alter the air and petrol adjustment.

I don't think I was nervous about coming down. I thought of that eventuality quite calmly and decided how I would glide down as near as possible to one of the dozens of naval vessels which I could see below me.

But the result of watching my engine closely was that I never saw the coast again and found myself well into France looking for my destination over absolutely unknown country.

Either by luck or by instinct I went straight to it—and then I did feel nervous really. I daren't throttle down the engine for fear of it stopping altogether, so I left the adjustment quite alone, shut off the petrol at the supply and glided down to 1,000 feet over the aerodrome; then opened the petrol again and the engine came on all right.

For the last little bit I used the thumb switch—making the engine buzz just now and again to give me sufficient speed to touch the ground in the required spot.

I put her down without breaking anything and felt extremely pleased.

When I landed I found a side-car driver of the squadron waiting about and asked if he had come for me. He said he had come for an officer who was flying over. 'That's me all right,' I said, and went down to the town for lunch.

After feeding I bought extra stars and had them sewn on my tunic and then came here.

I could not conceal from myself the eagerness I felt to get back. The side-car driver told me a few of the things that had happened since I was away—of the number of Huns down and the scraps with big formations, and of one of my flight missing—Donaldson, a comparatively new pilot here.

When I arrived I found that the side-car wasn't for me at all. Another pilot had had to fly an old machine that was being returned and the side-car was sent ahead to bring him back.

When he arrived and found I had taken his side-car he blasphemed for half-an-hour and wired for another.

I had quite a nice reception. The C.O.

and the Odd Man were playing tennis, and my flight was just starting on patrol. I offered to go, but the C.O. said it wasn't necessary.

Holt has done very well with the flight. He has got two Huns and two other fellows one each.

I started writing to you last night, but I was too tired and sleepy to continue. I slept until 7.30 this morning and was wakened then for patrol and the advanced landing ground. However, it was raining a little and was very overcast; and work is washed out for the day.

This gave me an early chance to tackle the C.O. I planted the MS. right on him and sat on his bed until he had read every word of the letters, and—I think—a lot more.

He said he saw no reason why it shouldn't go through all right and suggested a few minor alterations. And he liked it too!

So *now* you can go ahead. To-night I will post it with the C.O.'s written permission.

Just at this moment Holt, sitting on his bed, is deep in it and chuckling over your bits of humour.

Well, I think that's all the news I can think of.

I haven't said anything about my leave. But it isn't necessary, is it? It was just perfect.

And I love you.

BILL."

Many times I have read this letter. When I read it I like to recall his answer to my question, "You're coming back?... You *know* you're coming back?"

"I'm certain, quite certain," he said, didn't he, and you remember I was looking into his eyes at the time!

.   .   .   .

I also am unable to speak of our time together—except when I tell Joan of superficial details. I wonder if those who believe in Heaven could imagine anything more enthralling, more complete!

V

THE "little Saxon nest" is like a dream. The clear days of work and easy thought; the woods when, under the vivid green of the trees, bluebells grew so lavishly that they covered the dead brown leaves that in turn covered the damp earth—all these are distant, a lovely part of memory.

The ridge of the Downs against the sky will stay always before my eyes—so long I looked at it and prayed for my lover to come.

Molly and Nanny and the family of one are real; and some day I hope they will allow me to go back to them; but now I will go to Bill's people, who are my people—to stay with them till he comes again. To be with his sister is so sweet; to be with his mother will be sweeter still, for she gave him to me, and he is my life. Every day I thank her in my heart.

To-day's letter, though it is short, is very precious.

"My dear one," he says,

"By this time—2 p.m. Thursday—I think you will have received my wire about the C.O.'s approval of the book. Will you be glad?

I didn't wire you about my arrival because I hoped to let you know even the same day that the C.O. had given his approval, but I got here too late to tackle him.

I told you, didn't I, that Holt, who represents quite an intelligent reading public, was fearfully thrilled with the MS.

He read every word of it and loved your bits.

I am hoping to get a letter from you to-morrow, Friday, telling me of your journey and of your arrangement to go home with Joan.

The weather is wild and the clouds are low again, so I may go to the 'pool' this afternoon.

The record of 'Cheep' came and is quite good.

Will you send me my flying log-book. I left it by mistake in my hand-bag and I don't want to lose count of my hours.

It is a short letter to-day, for I have no news.

All, all yours.

BILL.

P.S.—In reading over the MS. with the C.O. I remembered how and why I had come to start one letter to you 'For whom I live.'

It was after I had had a letter from you in which you were troubled about Greta and also at a time when I had been having quite a lot of rather desperate scraps. I had wondered to myself why I had the luck to get through as I did, and it seemed to me I was just living for you as I wished.

Voila tout! I love you.

BILL."

VI

THIS afternoon we went into the enormous drawing-room which no one uses, and Joan played a nocturne of Chopin. It makes your heart weep.

I lounged in a deep chair with a picture before me of the evening, just about a fortnight ago when she played to us at home.

Bill's mother and dad were there—both content to have their boy again even for those few days, and glad to have me because I am his.

Near mother he sat, on the other side of the fireplace, twisting his pipe from one corner of his mouth to another, and whenever I looked up I found his eyes seeking mine.

Afterwards, when we were alone, he said:

"Aimée dear, did you *feel* me loving you?"

"Yes," I answered, for I think I am conscious of his slightest thought.

I wonder why I am so confident that he will come back to me? Every day I see the Roll of Honour and am forced to realize that there is no reason why I should be spared a grief that others have to bear just now.

And Bill's work is most constantly full of risk. Yet I am so perfectly at ease.

I think it is that I have faith in my own instinct and even more faith in his instinct; and he said:

"I'm certain—quite certain!" didn't he?

To-day's letter is rather disappointing, for he has had nothing from me since he left, and I wrote at once of course. But he knows that. I needn't fear that he would doubt that.

"Dearest one," he says,

"There was no letter from you to-day, but there is sure to be one to-morrow.

This morning I led the first patrol. It felt quite strange for the first twenty minutes. I couldn't feel the machine properly and couldn't tell where I was. However, it worked out all right and I kept a very good formation behind me.

We saw no Huns but got quite a lot of 'Archie.' At the end I landed at the advanced aerodrome with another fellow and stood by until 9 a.m., when we returned for breakfast; since I have slept until lunch.

Yesterday five of us took a tender to ——. We sat in a big French café for an hour and drank 'aperatifs,' and had a very good meal afterwards, with the wine you liked at the Savoy.

It was quite a decorous party, though I

completely lost my voice through singing 'rags' in the tender on the home journey.

There is another M.C. in the squadron—to Kelly. We are quite pleased, because though his judgment is not always good he is absolutely without fear and does his job always.

When I get your first letter I will have more to write about. I am longing to hear your reply to my wire.

All my love.

BILL.

P.S.—Don't worry about my flying logbook. I find I brought it after all."

I smile at that last sentence. It brings another picture to my mind—of our bedroom overlooking the sea, close to the golf links where we spent those glorious days away from the rush of town and all the people we knew, and seemed to barge into at every corner.

It was midnight, and Bill lay in a cosy chair with his feet on the bed, chewing his pipe and leisurely blue-pencilling the type-written copy of our book.

I stood about in my kimono,—having emptied all my belongings on to the floor,—wondering how I could cram all his golfing clothes into my suit cases.

As the problem seemed beyond me I went and sat beside his feet on the bed and, taking his pipe from his mouth, lighted a French cigarette from the glow under the ash.

Bill lifted his eyes from the book and smiled.

"I'm thirsty!" I said, smiling back.

"What would you like?" he asked—eager always to please me.

"Tea," I announced—looking at his watch and thinking how unreasonable was my wish, for it is not the sort of hotel that keeps its staff going in relays.

Yet for all that Bill went down and came back with tea, and for half-an-hour we drank it and discussed the four corners of the earth.

But while he was away I spied his precious flying log-book sticking out from the muddle on the floor.

Taking it up I kissed it and slipped it into the pocket of the haversack hanging on the post of the bed.

"That, at least, he must have if he leaves me and everything else behind," I said to myself.

And now he writes:

"Don't worry about my flying log-book... I find I brought it with me after all."

That is why I smile.

VII

At last we begin to talk properly. It seems rather one-sided until each answers the other.

Sometimes I am surprised that letters reach their destination at all these days, but, at other times I'm all impatience because of the loss of time between writing and being read.

"My darling," I read to-day,

"Ten minutes ago I was waiting on the aerodrome for the post to come in. It brought your first two letters.

Then I got into my machine and flew to the advanced landing ground. Now I am sitting under a haystack where I have just read your letters. They make me very happy—the one written in the train especially.

Last night I did a patrol and met nine Huns, but had no luck.

The first idea was to send out the whole squadron, but afterwards it was proposed that one strong patrol should go out, and that a few others should go out on their own and keep the patrol in sight.

Then, if a large formation of Huns was met they would be kept busy by our formation, while the odd roving ones, flying high above, might pick off a Hun or two.

Kyrle, Kelly, Hastings and I volunteered as the odd men and "B" Flight did the formation.

It was nearly a success, but just failed. After roaming about nearly three-quarters of an hour at 15,000 feet, the formation turned away up north just as nine Huns appeared from the east. Kyrle and Hastings went with the formation and Kelly and I were the only two who saw the Huns.

We manoeuvred against them for twenty-five minutes, and were within long range of them most of the time.

But I couldn't get near enough to fire, and was afraid to waste ammunition so far over.

Several times five of the Huns came directly underneath me, but two others were just above and I daren't go down, and at last, after we had worked a good way north we had to come away.

This morning I came to the advanced landing ground, but returned as it was perfectly dud. It cleared up a bit at lunch, so I have come out again, but there is nothing doing at all.

I shall go back for tea and to post this
to my wife.

And I send her all my love.

BILL."

Oh, how I wish I could be with him! It seems
such a waste for him to sit under a hay-stack
alone.

VIII

YESTERDAY morning, at the Hydro, we had
breakfast in our room. No letter had come from
Bill, but cheerfully I told myself it would arrive
by the afternoon post and would be more
precious for the delay.

About half-past nine Joan dressed herself
and was mending a tear in her "nighty" when
the maid knocked at the door and said one of us
was wanted at the telephone.

"Was it 'Mrs.' or 'Miss' they asked for?"
Joan enquired.

"Never mind which it was,".... I interrupted.
"I can't go down like this, so you'll have to go
anyway!"

Then I added so that she would hasten:

"Perhaps it's Dick—on leave!"

That sent her speeding away, and when she had gone I leant on my elbow and scribbled lazily at the beginning of the new diary for the second volume of our book.

Very soon she returned.

"They've been taken off—whoever it was," ....she grumbled..... "Isn't it silly?"

"They'll get on again," I said, not caring much, for I knew that if it were Dick he would persist.

Joan fidgeted about for a moment or two, then said:

"I think I'll go down to the lounge and write letters, and be handy if the 'phone goes."

"All right," I answered, adding: "If it's not too hot we might go for that walk, you spoke of.... I'll be down in half-an-hour."

As soon as the door closed I got out of bed, and after looking for some clean clothes began to brush my hair.

About five minutes later the handle turned.

"Who's that?... Is it Joan?" I asked.

The answer was indistinct.

"Wait a moment," I called, and, slipping on my kimono, unlocked the door.

She stood there. Her face was quite grey. I moved aside to allow her to come in, but I couldn't take my eyes from her eyes.

"What is it?... Oh, Joan, what is it?" I managed to say at length.

Then, as she seemed unable to speak, I caught hold of her hands.

"Joan—tell me what it is !" I cried.

"I can't... I can't," she began, and her voice was all broken up.

"It's not Bill?" I whispered—but of course I knew.

.   .   .   .

We packed our clothes. We would have liked to leave the silly things and run away at once, but of course we just had to go on being perfectly sane.

Joan was wonderful. She went and settled the account and gave our address for letters and asked the porter to send for the luggage.

Our one idea was to get to mother as soon as possible. We kept on hoping that dad had been with her when the wire came from the War Office; and sometimes I said that I knew Bill was all right—that he couldn't be otherwise because he had promised to come back.

After the first change of trains we travelled with a coarse fat woman in sweltering black clothes. With her were two small fat boys, also warmly wrapped in woollen garments.

As soon as we started one of them asked for a drink of water.

"I 'aven't no water, love," the woman said. "You've 'ad it all, you know quite well!"

"I want a drink of water," he moaned, and

kept on moaning in spite of her repeated assurances.

Very soon both were scarlet in the face, and the sweat was pouring from them.

The woman sat on the edge of her seat, as fat people often do; and in turn mopped her own and the child's forehead with a dirty handkerchief.

All at once Joan opened her bag and brought out some biscuits.

"Here you are," she said, persuasively. "That'll do instead of a drink, won't it?"

For a moment there was silence, while the other child, who had been sitting quietly watching nothing, grabbed his share and both stuffed their mouths as full as possible.

Then the thirsty one began again, for after his dry biscuits naturally he wanted his drink more urgently.

"You'll be 'ome soon.... 'Tain't many minutes now, love," the woman re-commenced, trying her utmost to console him—and then she turned to us to explain that they had come from Blackpool and had been on the way since early morning.

Soon after this a fight broke out. The one who wanted the water did it all, while the other one made placid efforts to shield himself.

After a few unheeded remarks the woman

picked the troublesome one up by his middle and plumped him on to the seat.

Defiantly he stared at her and slid off. Again she picked him up, and off he slid once more—staring solidly at her all the time.

I don't know what made us laugh—his expression or her persistence; but all at once we started to giggle, and soon the tears were pouring down my face.

I wanted to shriek with laughter and I wanted to howl with crying—but I managed to tell myself that if I started to lose control I might not be able to regain it.

Joan must have felt the same, for she stopped also.

By this time the child was howling lustily, for he had to be smacked very hard.

"I can't let 'im 'it the other one," the woman explained—panting now and purple... 'Ee would kill 'im... 'Ee would pull 'is eyes out, 'ee would."

.   .   .   .

The last word was said as we stood by the van on the station here waiting for our luggage.

"Hi!" we heard, and the call came so explosively that we turned without thought. The fat woman hung out of the compartment—her hat was awry and her face seemed as though it would burst through its skin—but she was looking beyond us to the porter.

"Hi!" she repeated. "'Oo's tin box d'you think that there is... that one on the platform?... You put it back where you took it from, you fat-head, or you'll 'ear about it, you will!"

The porter smiled, and calmly proceeded with his work.

"All right, mother," he said, "keep your 'air on.... Don't get 'ot or you might be sorry for it hafterwards!"

The woman's voice rose to a shriek.

"I'll keep my 'air on, you'll see, an' all!... In with that there tin box or they'll be trouble about. .. Fat lot it 'ud matter to you if I gets 'ome without me belongings... 'Urry with you, or by ——"

"'Ush, mother, 'ush.... See there it goes... Now be calm!" Saying this good-naturedly he heaved the tin box into the van again, adding:

"I wouldn't be *your* 'usband—not for something!"

Before the answer could be heard the whistle sounded and the train began to move. The woman had her last word, however.

We saw her at it, though we couldn't hear.

. . . .

Mother was there when we opened the door. Her face was smiling.

I couldn't bear that. She held me to her.

"I'm so glad you've come at last," she said.

"We're all hoping for the best... We're just hoping all the time."

Then she turned to Joan, and I went into the kitchen because it was the nearest place. Dad came and kissed me and went out again.

Bill dear, I knew you'd be sorry if I cried. I knew you'd think it utterly foolish.

Besides, you are coming back. You promised to come back. You *must* come back.

. . . .

We had tea.

Mother told us how she was alone when the telegram came and how she couldn't read it.

"I just kept the girl waiting there," she said. "I couldn't get it read."

The people next door sent for dad, and he hurried home at once on his bicycle—the bicycle you used when we were on Salisbury Plain, you know! It took you to the aerodrome in the morning and brought you home at lunch time; and then took you away again and brought you back in the evening—except when you crashed in that field and had to stay at the farm all night. But always it brought you back. I want to go on my knees beside it and kiss the pedals and the seat and the handlebars where you held them.

After a while dad had telephoned to us. Joan had said to him:

"I don't know how I shall tell Aimée....
I can't tell Aimée!"

Wasn't it like her to think of someone else
and not of herself?

. . . .

We read the telegram, and it seemed to give us
hope.

After all, many airmen have gone missing
and afterwards have been reported prisoners of
war.

Isn't it strange how much a matter of
comparison everything is?

Yesterday, before ten o'clock, to know that
you were a captive in a strange country where
we couldn't reach you; enduring hardships of
which we could know nothing; to contemplate
the days without your letters, would have
seemed unendurable; and to-day the news
would bring relief beyond all words.

About eleven o'clock we said good-night
and went to bed. The others looked so weary.
Their faces seemed to have become old and
colourless—almost without life.

I felt very wide-awake.

I slipped downstairs and found the St. Moritz
albums and brought them up to look at all
the snap-shots of you and at your Cresta Run
colours.

Joan was in bed with me—in the bed where
we slept together just two weeks ago; and when

we lay down she put her arm round me. Somehow she seemed so small and helpless that it made me cry. The tears trickled on to the pillow until it was wet.

I kept on remembering little things you had said and all your ways.

I love everything about you. You know how utterly I love you, dear!

Soon I felt I couldn't breathe and had to sit up.

And though you told me not to grieve if anything happened to you, I just couldn't stop crying.

Joan was crying too, then—quietly and helplessly like me.

She sat up and put her face against mine.

"Never mind," she whispered. "He's coming back... There's no need to worry. He's coming back!"

"I know," I sobbed, "I know he's coming back... He was certain of coming back—but I want him now—at this moment!... It's so lonely not to know where he is!"

After that we put on the light again and looked all through the albums once more and talked about the things you have done and how joyous you are and how lucky always.

But of course you would be lucky in any event. It's us who——. But we don't think of that... We know we shall see you again.

IX

DAD has written a lot of letters—among them one to Cox's to ask them to let us know if they should have a cheque, made out by you, from Germany.

And I have written a note to the "Odd Man" telling him how anxiously we hope to hear that you are a prisoner and even wounded. Darling, is it too selfish of me to want you in little pieces rather than not at all?

I want you with any sort of wound except one that will take your reason from you.

I will be your limbs—your eyes. I will be everything to you.

You said, didn't you, that you would find compensation always, and I know I could make you happy. We could live in Paris just the same, and we have our work together. Our love would be just wonderful. It is wonderful. You are my life. You are living for me, I know.

. . . .

Darling, although I can't send the letters, I feel I must write to you every day.

I want to tell you that I can't imagine life

without you. I can't believe you aren't alive. You seemed always to be just about twice as much alive as any of us.

To-day lots of letters have come—several of them from the squadron.

The C.O. and the "Odd Man" write so finally—as though they are certain you were killed. They say lovely things about you and your work, and speak as though only a knock-out blow could have sent you spinning down.

But Holt gives details.

He explains how you went out early on Sunday morning with several others, and how, when you were going up to meet some Hun scouts, which appeared unexpectedly after you had dived on to some others, the anti-aircraft shells burst in thick clouds, breaking up the formation. Suddenly you were seen to spin. For three thousand feet you were seen to spin— and then the others had to look out for themselves.

About an hour later Holt, at the advanced aerodrome, had a message from our anti-aircraft people that one of our machines had gone down out of control behind the German lines. They reported a wing missing, but those who were with you vow the machine was intact and think you must have had a direct hit.

He finishes, however, by saying that there is no reason to believe that if you were stunned you couldn't have regained consciousness in time to flatten out before hitting the ground.

All speak of your wonderful control over your machine and of the loss you are to the squadron.

That, knowing you, I can understand—but why do they have so little faith? Why is it left for us, here, to believe in you? I think death matters so little to them that, having gone from among them, you might as well be dead.

To me, too, death matters little—except if you are dead; and if you are I will come also.

As soon as possible I will learn to fly, and one morning early I will go up into the blue heaven and then let go! I will spin down and down, and down——!

Oh, if I could go up at once. If I could move—quickly—quickly... If I could go battling against the wind and gun fire and enemy machines.... If I could move—move all the while, I could grip this pain and laugh at it—and come to you very soon.

But here—Bill here in this house! Never to be alone—never to walk alone! To know, above all, your faith in me—that I should comfort mother and face her and all the world with perfect calm! It is too much. You couldn't realize how much you expected of me—you who had to go ahead always with your brain and your body!

Don't you know what you asked when you left me this to do? I think I can't go on.

X

DARLING—This morning I think you have broken some ribs?

Do you mind?

I think it because I dreamt about an umbrella with broken ribs.

It must be a code dream.

"Umbrella" is Morse or something for you.

I know you won't mind being an umbrella or any old thing just to please me.

Anyway you can have my ribs.

I have some extra ones, haven't I?

Or was it that you gave me some in the beginning?

Have them back, darling... Have them back at once! Really it seems immaterial which of us has them, because, as you know we are one.

Yesterday I pictured myself wheeling you in a bath-chair along a country lane, and then sitting down on the step by the wayside while we write a book.

How d'you like that? You can't possibly complain.

It would mean, of course, that you had come back with only one leg. Well, we can learn to walk beautifully with three, can't we?

You used only to have two legs before you married me, so you've gained one really. And even if you had none at all you would still have two!

.   .   .   .

Do you know what I have been thinking ever since we heard the news, and what I believe in most firmly except in those despondent moods which we all have because the tension is so great?

I believe that if you had been killed mother or I would have had some message from you— some sort of spiritual communion.

What it would be or how it would happen I don't know, but anyway it would be tangible to us whose thoughts never left you—never leave you—except in sleep.

This has nothing to do with any religious conviction, for, as you know, I have none except an idea that this can't be all we were created for.

I am convinced that you, who would be so eager to comfort us and to relieve our pain, would come to us in some way; and I feel that in some form you would stay with me and be my companion all the time.

Darling, everything about you is my

companion. I have no slightest wish apart from you. When you found me all the vague and ceaseless longing for "something, we know not what" left me—for you had come.

Dear, were two minds ever more in tune, or two spirits ever happier in the release—each to each? To be with you made the perfect night, the perfect morning—because all of you sought me, and all of me was yours.

How then could you leave me without a sign? You couldn't leave me so much alone.

XI

DARLING—Desirée has just gone. Yesterday she came to tell me she knows you are alive. She repeated what she had exclaimed after our marriage when she was feeling rather sore about it.

Do you remember—I told you?

She said:

"Before I saw him I hoped he would fall out of his aeroplane and break his neck... And now I've seen him I know that if he did fall out his neck wouldn't break!"

That, you know, was to announce her vexation, because, after having heard all her confidences and given her all mine since we wore frocks above our knees, I had dared to marry without telling her beforehand.

I understood, for I should have felt the same.

She repeated, too, what she had said when we all met in the Savoy lounge about three weeks ago—that she was convinced you would come through.

Her unreasonable confidence is life to me just now.

.   .   .   .

As she had travelled so far mother asked her to stay a night. She slept with me, and we talked for hours. She tried to persuade me to go back with her, but I told her I couldn't rest away from your people and that I couldn't leave them to wait for news of you.

Joan has decided to carry on with her work. So you see mother and I are alone most of the day.

This morning, very early, I lay thinking, and it dawned upon me that on this earth one *must* have some refuge which is not material. Life is too much master of the situation otherwise.

Here are we—or here am I anyway—unable to get away from the crude fact that I *must* have you back at any cost.

It is impossible—not that I should have you, oh no, not that—but the blank refusal to accept any alternative.

If I could believe in the survival of individuality after death; if I could be convinced that the spirit lives and is conscious of those who still must stay here; then I would be content to wait without your bodily companionship. I would know that by being true to you in word and thought and deed, I could keep you with me until my own spirit should leave this cage.

I could find strength to be kind to the others; to do my utmost to help mother and Joan and those who have depended on you for pleasure and interest. If I could believe this I could become—not outwardly resigned because I must show no surrender—but radiant, so that in seeing me all people could renew their hope. I could live most truly, as we are told to live, helping all with my double strength—yours, dear, and my own.

As it is, under this solid exterior, I am rebellious, full of self-pity and irritability. I am useless to the others. I am useless to myself.

The "Odd Man," in his letters, says: "God give you strength."

Bill dear—who is God?

He doesn't tell me that.

XII

DARLING—I want to live out of doors just now—all day and all night. I want to go to sleep under the sky and to wake under it. I want to see no houses and to have no walls about me. And I want the wind to blow and blow.

All the while I want to have a vision of you that is eluding me just now. All day I am with you. My last thought at night is yours. In the morning I wake and turn to you.

But I think under the open sky my spirit would find your spirit in the darkness—and that is what I want.

Perhaps you, also, are between four walls. Are you? Oh, send and tell us that you are! Send and tell us you are in a bed—a little hurt but not too much for your comfort, dear. And if you are in pain may I not come to you?

.   .   .   .

Last night I was impossible—utterly selfish and impossible.

Joan had been playing softly on the piano,

and you know her haunting touch. It was evening, and the sadness of the gloaming took hold of me.

Suddenly I cried, imperatively: "I want to go out."

Joan stopped playing.

"All right," she said; "I'll come with you in a minute."

"But I don't want you to come with me. I want to go alone," I answered.

"Oh, no!... You can't go alone," she exclaimed.

"Why can't I go alone?" I persisted. "I love being alone.... I hate always to be with other people!"

Poor Joan. You know how sensitive she is? I knew why she didn't want me to go alone, and it enraged me to think she should be afraid to leave me. Yet I realized my brutality and tried to soften it by adding:

"Take no notice of me to-night.... I'm bad-tempered!"

"You couldn't be bad-tempered, Aimée," she said most gently. "You're just tired that's all."

Bill, I could have screamed. I was afraid of myself.

Just then mother came in.

"Aimée wants to go for a walk alone," Joan said to her helplessly.

"No, I don't," I muttered.... "I did want to, but I don't now."

"Oh, no, you mustn't go alone," mother began.

"I tell you I don't want to go alone," I interrupted; then, from sheer inability to leave it there I began to argue.

"How can I work," I said, "if I never can be alone to think?... You can't think when others are with you all the time."

"Oh, but you don't want to work just now—not with your brain... We can't work with our brains just now," mother broke in.... "We can only just keep on—just keep on hoping from day to day."

Bill dear, I could have taken up all the things in the room and smashed them into tiny pieces—and the windows and the walls and the whole silly house!

"Joan will go with you.... She won't speak a word.... You'll be just the same as if you were alone!" mother continued—and then, mercifully, I saw her face.

I don't think that ever in my life I have seen anyone look so weary. I could have howled with crying over her. I didn't know what to do or say. I was ashamed.

I think we all sat under our juniper trees last night dear one.

XIII

To-DAY I said to mother:

"You know, dear, how convinced I am that Bill will come back to us because he said he would.... But I have been wondering what your religion would mean to you if you had to let someone go whom you love."

It was, perhaps, rather a cruel thing to ask, but I felt that if her belief meant anything she might be pleased to tell me and to let me share in her comfort.

She seemed willing to talk quite calmly.

She said she knows that those who are taken are alive in spirit always and conscious of us who are left.

"Then why do you grieve at the possibility of losing anyone?" I asked—adding: "If I had that belief I should be content.... Nothing could hurt me if I believed."

For a little while she was silent. Then she said:

"I grieve—I would grieve—just because I'm human, and I want to feel that those I love are on the earth... I want to be able to put my arms round my children... I'm a mother and I can't help being human, that's all."

Then I told her of the letter I had had from the "Odd Man's" wife.

"Whatever happens," she wrote, "it is no loss.... We have them always."

"What does she mean by 'no loss?'" I asked, worrying the problem to shreds because it all means words and nothing more to me; and I think that those who have come to some conclusion should be able to make it plain.

"I'm sure I don't know," mother said. "It is a loss, as we all know, if our dears don't come back.... I tell you it's because we're human it's a loss."

"Oh," I cried, for I wanted to solve the riddle and it wouldn't come right. "I don't believe in anything—and nothing you or anyone says makes me believe."

"Don't say that.... You don't mean it.... You can't mean that," mother whispered in a voice of pain.

"But I do mean it.... Can't you see that I'd give anything if I could believe—but I don't," I reiterated, stung and goaded by this stone wall of words, written and said!

Mother didn't speak for some time, and when she did it was to say:

"We must pray.... We must pray hard and we will get what we pray for... I believe that if I pray my boy will come back to me."

"Mother," I asked, quite desperately, "have all those who prayed and who believe had their dear ones back from this dreadful war?... Think of your own friends alone!... Have they not prayed?"

Again she was silent and then bravely she spoke.

"It's true," she said. "But whatever you say you can't take away my belief."

Ashamed of myself once more, I went and put my arms round her, kissing her.

"Darling," I whispered, "I don't want to take away your belief, but I just ache for you to give me some of it."

"It waits for all of us to see how we can stand the test," she answered tenderly. "But just pray, dear, and it will be easier... Just pray 'Thy will be done.'... That's what I'm saying all the time."

XIV

WE wait for the post on tenterhooks. Its no use objecting, Bill. We do. And telegrams are nightmares. When dad is away at work I open them because mother can't. That one from the War Office was too much of a shock.

Yesterday afternoon another came.

Mother had opened the door and she called to me. I rushed downstairs and took the envelope from her hand, tearing it apart. They must be read speedily, you know. We should find them unbearable otherwise.

This one said:

"Home on leave. Arrive to-night.— DICK."

Will you forgive me, dear? The tears blinded my eyes. You were so anxious for Dick and me to meet, and now it happens like this!

To mother, who had not seen her boy for two long years, it seemed like a miracle—a direct answer to one of her prayers.

.   .   .   .

He has come. I can't take my eyes from his face.

It isn't like yours in feature, really, but there is a look—a mannerism. And the voice is yours!

When he smokes his pipe—twisting it from one corner of his mouth to another and biting the stem, it is you!

He means just everything to us all just now. He is so perfectly optimistic. He says he simply *can't* be downhearted because he knows you'll come through all right. He whistles and sings ragtime, and brings a gust of life to this house.

After his bath, when mother and dad were tucked away in bed, he came into Joan's room and brought some French cigarettes.

Then we showed him the C.O.'s letter, which we hadn't dared to show to mother and dad because it seemed so final, and after all he knows no more than that you were seen to go down out of control. Dick read it slowly. At least it took him some time, because the smoke got into his eyes.

Then he said:

"What a doleful blighter!"

"Yes, isn't he?" I agreed.

.   .   .   .

Darling, Joan is playing ragtime for Dick's benefit.

I can't bear it. I think of the way you caught me to you when the music started and how, with our bodies close together, we danced and danced.

Bill, I can't picture the earth without you.

To have had you and to lose you,—it simply must not be!

I am utterly selfish. I want to come to you at once if you have gone.

What is this place without you? You didn't mean just this or that part of life.

My lover, my friend—everything! Always you said:

"Are you happy, dear?" or "Are you tired?" or "Do you wish for anything?"—and sweetest of all—"Do you love me, my wife?"

Yes, I love you, and I'm tired and I want to come to you, wherever you may be!

XV

DARLING—For three days I haven't written to you—and during those days I have faced the possibility that you may not come back.

It seemed to me that to have the full lesson of the trial we are enduring we must not shrink from any view of it. My thoughts have been muddled up with my emotion and it is difficult to separate the two.

Emotionally I feel I can't do without you. I *must* know your amazing need of me. My perfect artist—what should I do with my need which is your need?

Yet all else would I sacrifice for the delight or your clear brain—for the chaste, the unutterable satisfaction of your mental companionship.

There again we seemed to give and take with absolute equality.

To-night I make no feverish abandoned complaint. It's the waste that appals me. I can't get beyond that. Indeed I can't get beyond that.

.   .   .   .

To-day Dick took me, in a slow train, by the station you used when you went to the grammar school.

He showed me the old stone house where you lived then, and the path across the fields, where you ran every morning while the train grunted impatiently.

He showed me, too, the old seat where you spent hours with a notebook taking the numbers of the engines as they passed.

We hung out of the window together, and as the train moved Dick said:

"D'you notice those steps?... Well I can see him tearing up them always at the last moment—but never too late!"

I was wondering how they could allow any one else to use the steps after you, when he added quietly:

"He was my ideal then—and has been ever since.... All through these three years of war, if ever I've been in a tight corner I've said to myself: 'Bill's been in tighter ones and come through.' And that has brought me out all right; every time."

You see, dear, we all need you. You simply can't be spared.

.　　.　　.　　.

When we reached the town we went to book seats for a "revue." The others were to join us later and in the meantime we went to a little café—all corners and alcoves.

We tucked ourselves away, and over coffee and French cigarettes Dick talked of his time in Paris with you and of your days down the Seine on the skiff. And I told him of our marriage—for I know you wanted him to hear. He loved it all, and laughed so much at the bits which seemed most characteristic of you.

About six o'clock we met the family and arrived at the "revue" just after the curtain had risen.

The lights in the auditorium were low, and from then onwards, in that crowded smoky place, I saw you vividly. Never since the news came have I seen you so vividly. I heard what you would say as each one appeared on the stage and I heard your laugh.

Your stick, the one made from the broken propellor, with the band of the fragment of aileron control, was in my hand. It goes everywhere with me.

Suddenly—while in front of a black cloth a

number of girls were doing a ragtime dance—I saw *you* against the blue morning sky..... High up against the blue you were!... I saw the "Archie-bursts" around you.... I saw your machine stagger and begin to spin. I saw it spinning—down—down——.

And when it reached the ground, my heart stopped—to tear madly on again, for you stood up, and after saying "damn" quietly, just once, you fumbled in your pocket and brought out your pipe and tobacco pouch.

Dear, the pain of the blue morning sky overwhelmed me, but you—you are coming back!

XVI

TO-DAY is Sunday.

It is two weeks now since you went down.

This morning I made my usual pilgrimage to the bicycle shed to say my prayer.

I ask the old bicycle to bring you back again, you know.

This happens very early.

As soon as I wake, before I dress, I slip downstairs and out through the back door and along the little passage leading to the garden—

and then I come in and make the morning tea, for, by doing so, I keep everyone else in bed until the letters have arrived.

To-day it was later. I wakened with a start. The hands of the clock pointed almost to the time when they say you went spinning down. Springing from bed I ran to the kitchen and out to the garden, and as I went the sun came from behind a cloud. Most gloriously it came— enveloping me in a wondrous light. Suddenly the tightness left my heart.

"He is coming back.... He is certain to come back!" it sang. And I waited there, drinking in the promise thirstily until my brain and my spirit were revived.

Later we went to chapel.

It was mother's wish, of course. "If he's able to think at all, he'll picture us there this morning." And that stopped my hesitation.

We looked so cheery and festive that all miserable inquiry was squashed. People are kind, I know, but many seem to think it improper of us not to have red eyes.

I sat next to Dick, and showed him those three children who amused you so much. He bawled forth the hymns like you do, and then I opened the book at a place which said a lot about delight and blowing trumpets and joy coming after sorrow. It was lovely, and when we went out the day was lovely too.

. . . .

To-night mother told us all to go to bed.

When the house was quiet, Dick came into our room: and Joan and he and I have been sitting with you in the candle-light. We felt you so much with us and were so merry—in whispers.

Dick brought out a lot of French cigarettes that had fallen into his bath and had been dried on the cylinder.

We talked of you and Paris and St. Moritz and of the fun we shall have together afterwards.

All at once mother appeared. She was very cross.

We felt guilty and extremely young—but I was pleased to find that such a trivial thing had power to move her. We all seem more alive today. You must have been ill, and now you are out of pain!

.   .   .   .

Dear, we must wait. We know we must wait, and as mother repeats:

"We must go on hoping—just hoping all the time!"

For you said when I asked if you were coming back: "I'm certain—quite certain."

And I was looking into your eyes at the time.

You are living for me, I know.

PART III

I

AND so, after all, this *is* the end!

You who were certain of coming back, and I who was certain of it, too, have had to own ourselves completely baffled. On that Sunday morning your life went out "into the ether," and you left me here.

From higher than the highest hill you came spinning down.

Your body, that belonged to me, must have made a big hole in the ground.

And I, who could have rendered living beautiful for you, even if you had been crippled, or disfigured, or blinded, may not touch nor hear or see you any more. My useless tears are falling.

I can't believe that Life—the abundant share of it which was yours—could finish utterly; or that the individuality which made you mine could go back into nothingness again.

Yet, if that is not so, why did you—whose first thought was for me always—not come and make it known?

If anything that was you still exists, why don't you come now?

Why don't you come and take me too: or promise that I shall mate with you again?

Last night, in the darkness, I lay and realized what it means to be alone. And I thought:

"When he lay beside me before I spoke he knew my mood. I had no vaguest wish he didn't grant; no problem he didn't solve; no pain he could not soothe.... My pleasure was his pleasure; my sorrow he took from me.... And now when the greatest of all sorrow has come through him he doesn't speak."

That *cannot* be his wish.

What does it mean?

.   .   .   .

Well, dear, that's over!

And now I'm going to pretend.

I'm going to pretend from this moment that you are alive and with me all the time.

I'm going to pretend that you never leave me night or day; that we are as much together as we were when I could see and touch and hear you.

If there should be spells when this is not satisfactory entirely we will laugh them away— or if laughing doesn't act we will discuss them seriously as our habit is.

I've been thinking of how many women must be feeling alone just now, and I wondering how they tackle the situation.

Some, I suppose, have a definite religion to see them through. They will bow their heads and say to their God:

"Thy will, not mine, be done!"

Others must be rebellious, and are spending their vitality in a fury of pain which time will wear down to resignation.

Others, who married because marriage happened to come their way, will find consolation from expressions of sympathy and from the dramatic possibilities of mourning.

Those who, like me, have had to renounce what made them whole—the someone before whose coming they were consciously incomplete, and at whose coming they became as, consciously, complete,—will face the inevitable according to their ability, until the time comes, when they too go out into the "nothingness" or to the "everything" that must come eventually.

At first they may believe—as I believed—that nothing would do except to follow at once—at once: that they must force Death to pause in his greedy harvesting and gather them too—but a small voice may whisper to them also:

"Death knows his own business.... If you tamper with your Destiny you may miss him whom you seek.... It is all too incomprehensible for you to interfere!"

II

GOOD-MORNING, Bill!

You see I say "Good-morning" just as though you hadn't been with me all night!

You have been, of course; but I shall chatter like this on paper because I can't go about speaking out loud in any other way—and you know how I love to hear my own voice?

Such a lot of things happened yesterday, and you were with me through them all.

I found myself smiling at your remarks especially in chapel—but we'll talk of that in a minute, for first I must explain why I don't speak of how the family are taking the final news of you. I don't speak of it simply because they don't know—because they haven't received it.

The, Odd Man wrote to me—and I simply can't speak of it so soon! Before the post came I had put the kettle on the gas, and had been out to the bicycle shed to say my prayer for your return.

Then, while the kettle boiled, I read the letter; and afterwards hid it away in my kimono sleeve—and there you are!

Mother goes on "hoping—just hoping all the time," and if you think I ought to have told her you will understand that these few days before the official word comes can't make much difference to her—and that I *must* have them to myself to bury my dead. By "my dead" I don't mean you, dear. You are living for me and with me all the while I know. I mean the idea of the tangible "you"; for it takes a little while to lay upon the altar of whatever power there is the something which seemed so essential to our staying here at all—the body, the touch, the kisses, the human presence! It takes a little while to force our lips to say:

"Thy will, not mine, be done." Especially when we don't know whose will we mean.

That's why I guard my secret; why I listen unmoved when they speak of you as a prisoner of war; when Joan comes home with another story of someone whose husband or son has written after many weeks; or when mother says: "We'll send him such lovely parcels, see if we don't;" or, "If we could just see his name on a cheque, that would do for us, wouldn't it?"

And if, when I may have failed to answer and she repeats "Wouldn't it, Aimée?" I say "Yes, mother!" it is because I must; knowing all the while that no signature of yours will be seen by us any more.

That's why I come up here to my attic to be alone with myself—and you.

. . . .

On going downstairs at lunch time yesterday I found Mr. Blair in the dining-room.

As a previous minister of the chapel he had travelled to make his speech at the formal welcome to the new man, and had come first to hear the latest news of you, whom he chooses to call "one of his boys."

When Joan and dad and "the kid"—who, by the way, goes on, in the back garden, playing at air-battles as though you had not fought your last; and at artillery duels as though Dick were not risking his life in one at this moment—had gathered at the table, and mother had served the food from her place at the end, we ate and laughed a lot about nothing, and then I went into the kitchen to see to the coffee.

While it was going through the process of being made I, having done no work except to cover up one bed and "brew" the morning tea, "washed up"; and as usual, quite valiantly you did your bit—which was to stand about filling your pipe, urging me to hurry and come and have a cigarette instead of wasting time poking about in a pan of greasy water.

Didn't I always agree most heartily when you vowed you never would wish me to do any housework of any sort whatever—except to make coffee, that being an aesthetic pleasure to us both. At last, having carried in the tray and handed round the cups, I slipped away to go up to the bedroom where I lay appreciating, with you, the humour and quaintly expressed truth of "A Knight on Wheels," by Ian Hay.

You remember Dick wanted us to read it! And I knew, when you said "it's so very sane," that you meant the way the writer views life over the top of pre-conceived ideas.

Presently Joan appeared.

"Dad's gone and mother's asleep and Mr. Blair wants you to come and give him a few hints about publishers.... He has some writing he wants to see in print," she announced.

Lazily turning over, I answered into the pillow: "Tell him I don't know a thing about publishers. I've met only one and I don't know anything about him except that he lives with his mother."

At this Joan seated herself on the edge of the bed. She's much too wise to try to coerce anyone.

"I'd rather stay here myself, too," she said, knowing quite well that she would be obliged to go and talk if I didn't.

I knew it too and yet I said:

"Go down and give him the address of the

man upon whose advice one can rely... And then come back here as quickly as you can."

Just as I finished speaking, darling, you interfered.

"That's not fair," you whispered. "Besides, old Blair is quite good fun—not a bit a preachy sort.... And he thinks no end of me"—you added, with one of your occasional touches of self-appreciation.

After that you can imagine it didn't take me long to hop out of bed. I slipped into my dress and powdered my nose and tidied my hair and was down in two minutes.

Mother lay dozing on the sofa. Mr. Blair sat by the grate smoking a cigar and, when Joan and I had fitted ourselves into the big armchair, in low voices we discussed books and manuscripts and the placing of work; and then the talk worked round to you.

"Everything was as easy as could be to him," said Mr. Blair. "Without a bit of trouble he just carried away all the prizes at school—but he never cared.... *We* got excited, he didn't!

"Yes," agreed Joan, "he always seemed a bit aloof from it all, in spite of being so jolly and all that."

As they said this, darling, a wave of remembrance of your complete giving of all of yourself came over me. Nothing you kept back— nothing you held aloof. Just all of you was mine and all I took.

Now, as I sit here, I recall, too, something that occurred in our bedroom overlooking the golf links by the sea.

I had spoken some half-formed wonder that you should go on caring for me as you did. It was just the whimsical statement of a woman who can't let well alone; for truly I knew that with our conception of life and of each other, our union would grow with the years. Eagerly you came to me.

"Dear, you are mine always," you whispered, making me meet your eyes—and then your voice became more calm.

You held my hands:

"I should have said," ... you continued quietly and with grave confidence, ... "that *I* am *yours* always—all, *all* yours."

.   .   .   .

Well, to get back to yesterday, Bill, old boy!

At three o'clock mother invited and resented criticism upon the angle of her hat; then went with Mr. Blair to chapel to hear the first sermon of the day.

"Hurrah!" cried Joan in the tone of voice that reminds me of you when, every now and then, you decided to get a hundred seconds out of a minute, "we've three hours and a half all to ourselves . . . . What shall we do?"

"Three hours and a half?" I queried. "How's that?" She snatched up a leaflet from the table.

"See here;—Service, by Mr. What's his name three thirty until five.... Tea in the school-room five until six thirty—ninepence.... Fancy they can eat for an hour and a half for ninepence, and in war time, too!" she rattled on fatuously. Her mood was infectious, and feeling gloriously irresponsible we rammed our hats on our heads and let off steam by a quick tramp over the fields: then, coming home again, we shed our outdoor clothes and lounged about in kimonos, making tea and collecting from tins in the larder all the nice things to eat.

We were too late for the second service, of course, and the ministers, who were to address us, already filled the place where the choir usually sits, under the pulpit facing the congregation.

With them was the mayor who, after a few jokes and a few sensible remarks about the practical side of religion, apologised for handing the chair over to a deputy—because he had to attend several other meetings in the town.

When he had trotted away and when the vestry door had closed upon him, the deputy introduced another "brother," who stood up and, rather unexpectedly, began to pray.

I couldn't decide whether to kneel or not, so, as there was nothing to kneel upon and I was wearing the costume you like so much, I just leant my forehead against the edge of the pew in front and talked to you.

The brother's voice was oddly pitched, and he played about with some of his words and once you exclaimed: "Oh, fids!" which made me giggle, and at that the woman in front sat up and nearly knocked my hat off.

You see, we had a tolerably exciting time.

Then, darling, the girl with the contralto voice went on to the platform and sang. To the accompaniment of the organ she put her heart and soul and all her lovely tenderness into her song.

We were close together, dear heart—and when she finished with "Ships that pass in the night," I held you very firmly, for we didn't just "speak each other in passing," did we?

We became one, and you are with me evermore.

A thought has just whispered to me that when I die you will be waiting, as you did at the marriage office; and you'll come forward, as you did then—so eagerly and tenderly—and you will take my hands and say "Aimée."

Oh, I wish Death would hurry and come this way! One extra couldn't make much difference to him when he is taking such crowds and crowds. And if he must have an exact number, couldn't you persuade him to spare someone who wishes to stay here, and to take me instead?

Couldn't you go to him and say: "Look here, old man, I've left my wife across there. I don't want her to think I've forgotten about her. Perhaps you wouldn't mind just putting back your old skiff a moment—and if there's anything we can do for you, don't mind asking!"

If he's a decent sort at all, Bill, that should be enough; but if he seems inclined to stand on his hind—I mean, on his dignity—just say "Sir" instead of "old man," and perhaps "ferry boat" or "launch" instead of "old skiff."

There's no sense in getting his back up and taking any risks.

I'm not grousing, Bill. It's only a suggestion, and if it doesn't meet with your approval, I'm ready to admit that you were right most times. If you decide that there are things to be done here for a while, I'll stand to all right, you know.

.   .   .   .

But all this time I'm trying to tell you that the meeting at least gave me an insight into the "other person's" point of view, for I heard enough to convince me that while I could find a

God more easily up here in my attic with you, or out in the country where the sun shines and the wind blows, some can get beyond what seems to me a muddle of words that hinder thought rather than develop it. When a minister said, with an earnest wish to spread his conviction:

"God is in Heaven," I wanted to ask, just to begin with:

"Is God like Bill?" For really when you come to sift it out the only God any of us can understand is our Most Beloved, and the only Heaven any of us desire is to be with our Most Beloved without fear of parting or of love becoming less.

Can any of us, with our human comprehension, get beyond that?

III

LAST evening when Joan and I returned from a long tramp over the high fields against a stiff wind, mother, who had been baking bread and now stood at the kitchen table, said:

"Dad's in the dining-room."

"Alone," said Joan, briskly.

"No," he's not alone.... He's with ———."

"Oh, I know! With old Methuselah what's-his-name!"

"Now, Joan," censured mother, "don't you be so quick. You're too brisk by far now-a-days. You don't know who dad's with, so let me speak!"

"Sorry, mother," said Joan, giving her a jaunty kiss." Go ahead! Who is it?

"You're so quick, you never let me open my mouth," continued mother, quite aggrieved and unable to proceed.

Joan smiled at her and going to the sink began to pull a lettuce to pieces without waiting to take off her hat.

"There you go, and you'll spoil that skirt, too," chided mother seeing her unrepentant.

"All right, I'll cover it up," said Joan agreeably, unhooking an apron from the peg, and adding, as she did so, "I'm sure *I* don't care who's in the dining-room ... I'm hungry. I want some food."

At this, perversely, after a little pause, mother said:

"It's the man who was in Paris for a fortnight—the one Bill showed round."

Suddenly Joan stopped splashing the lettuce leaves, and began to laugh.

"Oh, Aimée," she cried, "it's that man who

went from here! ... The one dad gave Bill's address to. You remember I told you. Bill wrote home: 'What on earth have you sent out this time. He doesn't smoke or drink; he doesn't like music or theatres—and he's never spoken to a woman in his life!'"

And I wrote back on a postcard: "Don't bother about the man. He's no special pal of ours."

And, of course, Bill left it lying about, and the man may have read it, for one day he handed it to him, saying, "This is yours, I think!"

.   .   .   .

But here again, Bill, I had an insight into the other person's point of view, for when, after supper, we went into the dining-room to please mother, the man, with a break in his voice, spoke of his time in Paris as the happiest of his life.

You were so good to him, he said.

Being un-adventurous he mentioned with awe your airy disregard of most things— especially your own safety.

"He had so many narrow escapes," he finished, wishing to comfort us in our anxiety:

"He'll come out of this all right, you'll see. He's such a lucky chap."

"Well, that's what we believe," said mother. We're hoping for the best.... We're just going on hoping all the time."

Then it was, dear, that I wanted to say quite calmly: "He's lucky still.... He's dead." But the words didn't come; and realising that I had done, as usual, less than my share of housework that day I rose and went into the kitchen to wash the supper dishes.

. . . .

I've been to the dentist.

If you've got to stay on this planet you can do it more pleasantly without a hole in your tooth, can't you?

After gagging my mouth and putting that grinding thing right into the roots of my head he said, working away at the wheel:

"Now, just raise your left hand if I hurt you!"

I thought:

"My son, it would take more than this to make me sing out now-a-days.... I'm fireproof, more or less."

But I daresay if he had been too familiar with a pet nerve it would have been just as hateful as it used to be.

Life's rather amusing—taking it all round.

IV

BEYOND doubt the greatest difficulty is mother.

Mothers, it seems, have no interests of their own. They see life through their children, and what happens when, as now, their children go away and come again no more.

What can we do for them?

I, Bill dear, feel very helpless. I'm so impatient, too. Always I have wanted other people's way to be my way—and not mine theirs.

Small restrictions irritate me to impatience —and yet one must be above impatience, of course.

Because of this irritation in myself I find it perilous to talk below the surface of things to mothers. My tone, and the fact that they are unaccustomed to argument, make discussion seem like a personal attack. And yet I know of no way to friendship except discussion, and without friendship how can one be of use?

I wish I had your big calm way. Perhaps if I pretend enough that you are expressing yourself through me I may conquer my futility.

.   .   .   .

Yesterday we went into the park.

"That," said mother, nodding toward a circle of grass, "used to be a cricket ground.... Many a time we spent an afternoon here, before the war, watching them play... We had county matches and all, you know," she finished, so that I shouldn't imagine it to have been merely a provincial playing field.

When we had admired the circle of cultivated grass, and walked on again in the sunshine she continued:

"You should have seen them—how lovely they looked in their white clothes against the green all round!"

Overjoyed by the picture she visualized—of the players with their alert bodies springing upward to catch a ball; or running and bending with the grace that balanced muscular development gives—I smiled, and was smiling still when she cried in a voice full of rebellion:

"It's a shame—it's a dreadful shame to think of so many of them killed and gone!"

I traced a pattern on the ground with your stick, Bill dear; and I answered, musingly, unguardedly:

"I don't know... Is it a shame?"

Incredulously she turned to me.

"Not a shame... And them so young and full of health?"

Having started I went on:

"Death has to come some time... It must be lovely to die when you're most full of life," I said.

"But do you think *they* would have chosen to die?... They who could have lived many a happy year!" she persisted, hardly crediting my words, I think.

I answered:

"No one chooses to die—or very few of us; but who is to say that the years would have brought happiness to them?... It isn't certain, is it?"

Mother seated herself on the bench beside which we had stood.

"Then you don't think this war is a terrible thing?" she asked.

Quickly I answered her, able to agree at last.

"I think war is a senseless and horrible mistake—and I think if there is a God he must weep for our stupidity.... But it's us who are to be pitied, isn't it—not those who are dead," I said.

Mothers are so very sweet—and so pathetic. I wish we could help them!

V

BILL dear, last night I felt wonderfully happy.

Joan was asleep. I had been reading, and afterwards, in the darkness, had no wish for sleep.

You were with me. I was content. How can I explain it?

Not many days and nights ago I cringed from the very suggestion that you might not come to me again as I had known you hitherto.

That you could be with me after I no longer could touch your body or hear your voice seemed too incredible to bring even the vaguest sense of comfort.

I felt too forlorn—too alone.

Now, without reason, beyond all argument even of my own making, I know that you are mine, that you are *me*, more completely than when I lay in your arms breathing the breath from your mouth that touched my mouth.

On looking back it seems that upon our most holy moments there fell a shadow—a shadow cast by the knowledge of human chance and change; of partings and vague fears.

We two faced living with so much to make

us courageous and buoyant—but I, for one, was afraid.

I was afraid of Sorrow.

I would have gone a long way round to escape meeting Sorrow face to face.

And now that he has taken me by both hands and has forced me to stand and meet his gaze, I find I am looking into your eyes; that it is you who hold my hands; you who whisper that you will go with me to the end of this earthly journey helping me to fulfil the tasks that destiny has pre-arranged; that it is you who will gather me into your being when the last task is done.

You are God now, for your human body has released your spirit that is one with the great spirit of Love.

Oh, I realize acutely the limitation of words. I see why symbols, worn out and ill-conceived, are voiced by those who would give spiritual guidance to others who grope with Reason for a light in their blindness!

There are no words. The revelation is beyond speech. Neither music nor sunshine, nor the wind on a mountain, could convey the joy of it.

That is a pity—for just now so many beat their unseeing eyes as I beat mine a short while ago, and I would like to share my faith.

But what do you whisper?

"Let all, when they must, meet sorrow face

to face.... Let them stand as you stood, blinded by tears—and when the tears are passed they shall see, and have no more fear...
...In the meantime let your love, your happy love, reveal that we who are dead are living with you all, all the while.... Just carry on.... We'll see you through."

Thank you, Bill.

THE END

There is no death but forgetfulness;
everything that has loved and has
loved to the end will meet again
                              MAZZINI

ANNOTATIONS

PAGES

9 line 1. The date was April 11th 1917.

15 line 18. A Nieuport 17 Scout, a recent replacement for their late and unlamented FE8 pushers.

16 line 2. 'Hyatt'—actually Lt. Herbert Edward Oscar 'Bill' Ellis MC, a personal friend with whom Bond had served at Suvla Bay and in France. In April and May 1917 Ellis claimed six enemy aircraft destroyed, plus one shared OOC. He was injured in a crash on 6.5.17, lost much of his memory and was forthwith invalided home.

21 line 14. Bond's first operation was on 13.4.17 in his usual aircraft B1545.

25 line 6. First offensive patrol on 14.4.17 with Lt. K. Mackenzie (later referred to as 'Duff') and 2nd Lt. S. Thompson.

27 line 15. 'Captain Romney' was Captain William Robert Gregory MC, son of Sir William and Lady Augusta Gregory of Co. Galway, Ireland. Gregory had probably been responsible for shooting down the German ace Manfred von Richthofen on 6.3.17. Educated at Harrow and Oxford, Gregory was old (35)

for a fighter pilot. A good cricketer and boxer, he was also a more than promising painter and designer. Married with a son and two daughters, he later commanded 66 (Camel) Squadron, and was KOAS (killed on active service) in Italy in January 1918. Bill describes his character on page 127.

33 line 21. 19.4.17. The other 'fellow' was Lt. K. Mackenzie.

33 line 29. The 'fellow' was 2nd Lt. Edward 'Mick' Mannock, later to become one of Britain's foremost fighter aces, with some 61 aerial victories. Aimée later referred to him as 'Kelly'.

42 line 8. Though I have carefully checked all the reference books on English Follies, I can find no trace of this one. It may possibly be 'Fritham's Folly' in Hampshire.

45 line 22. The date was 22.4.17.

49 line 21. The date was 23.4.17.

50 line 3. The British Nieuport 17s were armed with a single drum-fed Lewis machine gun mounted on the top plane above the pilot's head via a fixed mounting devised by Sergeant R.G. Foster of 11 Squadron. The fixture allowed the weapon to fire forwards and slightly down-wards over the tip of the airscrew blades using a Bowden cable trigger and a telescopic Aldis gunsight. The drum only carried 97 rounds, hence a pilot might have to reload during combat, a procedure which involved pulling down the Lewis, disengaging the empty pan, and fitting a loaded replacement, a

manoeuvre often carried out during a whirling dogfight! There was the remote possibility of a drum slipping from the pilot's hands, and striking him on the head, and at least one unfortunate 40 Squadron flyer pulled the loading wire of the gun by mistake, whereupon the weapon slid down and the gun butt caught him a stunning blow on the helmet! On the plus side the Lewis could be pulled down to fire upwards into an unsuspecting opponent's belly.

50 line 15. C.F.S.—Central Flying School.

51 line 3. The near-vertical dive was necessary as Nieuport pilots had to aim their Lewis guns 15 degrees above their line of flight, using the Aldis sight, in order to hit their opponents. German airmen simply had to fire along their line of flight, with their twin Spandaus which were synchronised to shoot through the propeller arc.

54 line 12. On 24.4.17 two 40 Squadron pilots, Lts. J.G. Brewis and I.P.R. Napier, assisted by a Naval Sopwith Triplane, forced an enemy DFW CV two-seater to land at Le Façon, near Béthune, ten miles on the British side of the lines.

55 line 3. On 25.4.17 the squadron relocated to Auchel.

58 line 14. Captain F.R. Barwell. Sadly this officer was KIA (killed in action) on 29.4.17.

62 line 19. On 29.4.17 the squadron moved to Bruay, a short distance south-east of Auchel.

63 line 5. This was the Lt. Brewis who had helped to

bring down the DFW on the 24th.

65 line 21. Bruce Bairnsfather (1888-1959) was an artist who served as an officer on the Western Front. He became famous for his cartoons and sketches of trench life, which were later published in a series of books. His most popular creation was the veteran front-liner 'Old Bill.'

65 line 26. The squadron's Nieuports were not camouflaged, being left in their natural silver-doped finish.

68 line 1. The balloon strafe took place on 2.5.17. The crew of the kite balloon attacked by Bill both baled out, and although the inflatable failed to ignite, it was thoroughly riddled and collapsed and fluttered earthwards under his fire. Lt. Mackenzie's Lewis gun was the one that jammed.

70 line 9. Presumably Portsmouth, which makes 'Fritham's Folly' (page 42) more likely.

71 line 3. The 'Odd Man', a most remarkable chaplain, according to Bond, was named by William MacLanachan in his *Fighter Pilot* as 'Padre Keymer' but little else is at present known about this singular personality. See Bond's comments concerning him on pages 72-3 and 199.

71 line 22. Captain Albert Ball, a famous 44-victory ace. On this date, 26.4.17, he was credited with two victories.

75 line 23. The CO of 40 Squadron was Major Leonard

Arthur Tilney MC, an Old Etonian and 22-year-old combat veteran. He was KIA in March 1918. See Bond's brief description of the '*tousle-headed youth*' on page 80.

79 line 3. The date was 6.5.17.

81 line 26. On 7.5.17 a second balloon strafe destroyed six of the enemy inflatables, but Captain William Eric Nixon, a new arrival to the unit, was shot down. He was, like Bill, born in Derbyshire, and I devoted a chapter to him in my *Winged Warriors*, published in 2003.

82 line 13. Obviously one of Bill's old flames, and of whom Aimée was quite naturally suspicious.

83 line 26. This action took place on 10.5.17.

85 line 1. This aircraft may have been from *Schasta* II, one of whose machines crashed at Sailly en Ostrevent on this day.

88 line 11. Captain Arthur Willem Keen MC, a 14-victory ace, crash-landed just behind the British front line on 13.5.17. He became CO of 40 Squadron in 1918, and was severely burned in a flying accident in August, dying in September of that year.

92 line 10. The 'new pilot' was Canadian 2nd Lt. Albert Earl Gregory, in due course a 14-victory ace and referred to by Aimée as 'Grahaeme.' Bond gives a marvellous description of him on page 169 in one of his letters.

94 line 24. The 'Air Hog' was the larger-than-life Welshman 2nd Lt. Lewis Langharne Morgan who gained his soubriquet for his manic zeal in engaging the enemy. He was awarded the MC for his *general keenness and good work* but lost his right leg below the knee after being hit by German ack-ack on May 24th. Despite his injuries he returned to flying, rejoining the RFC in 1918. This unconquerable fighting man died when the motor of his SE5 failed on take-off from his 50 Squadron base in April. He deserved a better fate.

97 line 25. 'Dick' was the pseudonym for Bill's brother, Sergeant Alfred Ernest Bond MM, RFA. Bond visited him on 16.5.17 and met up with him on several subsequent occasions.

109 line 29. The squadron was No.1, then stationed at Bailleul.

110 line 2. 'The Hun' or 'Haystack Expert' was 2nd Lt. John Lancashire Barlow. His second nickname arose as a result of his first flight with 40 Squadron on 20.5.17 when he hit an inoffensive heap of straw on take-off. On his second flight he landed heavily, careered between a hangar and some cottages and ended up on his nose in a sunken road, hence his first nickname. A colleague later wrote that Barlow *treated the war as if it were really a rag on a stupendous scale.* He went on to claim six victories with the unit, before he was killed on a patrol in September 1917. He was only 18-years-old.

120 line 2. 'Harvey'—obviously another pseudonym—was evidently a former flame of Aimée's,

seemingly disabled during the war.

129 line 2. Douai. Date 27.5.17.

129 line 9. Somain.

129 line 13. Henin Lietard.
133 line 11. 'Last night' was 28.5.17.

145 line 22. 'Allison' was Captain W.T.L. Allcock, the date 1.6.17.

147 line 21. The wounded pilot was Lt. W.E. Bassett, the date 1.6.17.

148 line 19. 3.6.17. Gregory ran out of petrol and landed at Bertangles.

148 line 27. The effects of constant high flying without oxygen may have affected Bond's judgement, and pilots who flew in the Great War have commented on the symptoms that a lack of oxygen may have produced on some aviators, leading to poor landings and other sorts of defective flying.

155 line 11. The date was 4.6.17 and the enemy airfield was Douai.

158 line 6. The Triplane was probably from 'Naval 8' Squadron RNAS, stationed at nearby Mont St Eloi.

162 line 3. This combat took place on 5.6.17. The two pilots who had to return with engine trouble were Lt. J.W. Shaw and 2nd Lt. William MacLanachan, who was later to score 7 victories with the unit.

163 line 1. Bond's victim may have been Lt. Oskar von Schickfuss und Neuhoff, cousin of the Red Baron's mother, whose Albatros crashed near Monchy on that day.

163 line 18. 'The other two' were 2nd Lt. Herbert Bolton Redler, later called 'Holt' by Aimée, and Godfrey. Redler scored 10 victories in the war, and was killed in a flying accident in June 1918.

165 line 18. The new advance, which commenced on 7.6.17 was on Messines Ridge.

167 line 16. The missing pilot was Lt. J.W. Shaw.

172 line 17. Lieut. G——(Godfrey), Lieut. B—— (Bond).

179 line 8. The combat took place on 9.6.17.

180 line 3. 'Scott' was 2nd Lt. L.B. Blaxland.

182 line 15. We know very little about the early life of Aimée McHardy, apart from information gleaned from the Scottish birth and census records. She was born in July 1886, daughter of William Arnot McHardy, a Scot, and Mercy (née Baker) who was English. He was described as a commercial clerk, and the family lived in the Kelvin district of Glasgow. By the time of the 1891 census Aimée and her sister Maude were living with their Aunt Fanny Baker in Glasgow, who is presumably the lady mentioned on page 182 line 9. By the time of Aimée's marriage in 1917 the family had moved to Oxford Street, St Marylebone, London, though by this time her father, described as a salesman

in dyestuffs, was dead. The family had evidently come up in the world as Aimée mentions the employment of servants at their Oxford Street home.

184 line 7. 'Faulkner' was 2nd Lt. B.B. Lemon.

187 line 19. The place was Douai, the date 12.6.17.

187 line 30. The Squadron was No.10.

194 line 23. The date was 16.6.17, and the 'other fellow' was Lemon.

194 line 27. The town was Lille.

195 line 2. The town was Tourcoing.

203 line 3. This took place on 18.6.17.

208 line 25. The test took place at Mount St Eloi.

210 line 25. Lieut. B——(Bond).

211 line 1. Lieut. G——(Gregory).

225 line 1. Bond's leave commenced on July 2nd 1917 and ended on the 19th.

229 line 11. The 'Hydro' was probably at Buxton in the Derbyshire Peak District.

231 line 6. 'Joan' was Leila Bond, Bill's elder sister.

234 line 10. The aircraft referred to was most probably a Sopwith Camel.

237 line 20. 'Donaldson' was 2nd Lt. G. Davis.

243 line 20. The other 'fellow' was Lt. H.A. Kennedy.

247 line 5. 'Hastings' was either 2nd Lt. G.L. Lloyd or 2nd Lt. F.W. Rook.

253 line 27. The Bond family lived at 19 Tennyson Avenue, Chesterfield, amazingly directly across the road from Derbyshire's leading World War I fighter ace, Captain Edwin Swale, DFC and bar (17 victories), who lived at no. 22.

258 line 11. Although Redler wrote to Aimée, the most convincing description of Bill's death was given by William MacLanachan in his book *Fighter Pilot*, first published in the 1930s. He recounted the events which took place on an early morning five-plane patrol on Sunday July 22nd which was heading back over the lines at Lens when a series of shellbursts scattered the formation. Bill's B1688 took a direct hit and was literally blown apart. '*All that remained in the air*', wrote the Scotsman, '*were the stupid dancing remnants of his planes.*' Redler too was hit, and the engine cowling was literally torn off his machine. He was however able to crash-land just behind the British front-line trenches. The squadron was devastated by Bond's loss, MacLanachan commenting that, '*The fact that the indomitable Bond had been killed by a direct hit from Archie meant more to us even than the loss of a friend.*'

274 line 10. Staveley Netherthorpe Grammar School.

275 line 17. The theatre was probably the Hippodrome

on Corporation Street, Chesterfield, which staged a 'novelty review' entitled 'Wait a Minute' in August 1917.

290 line 22. The mayor was Sir Ernest Shentall (1861-1936), Councillor, Alderman and Mayor of Chesterfield 1913-18.

298 line 3. The cricket ground was Queen's Park, Chesterfield, one of the prettiest grounds in the country, and where Derbyshire played county matches for a hundred years, between 1898-1998.

COMBAT CLAIMS

CAPTAIN
WILLIAM ARTHUR BOND
MC and bar

DATE	AIRCRAFT FLOWN		LOCALITY	ENEMY	CLAIM TYPE
2.5.17	Nieuport 17 B1545		Noyelles	Kite balloon	Destroyed
10.5.17	,,	,,	SW Douai	Aviatik	Destroyed
13.5.17	,,	,,	Douai	Albatros CIII	OOC*
28.5.17	,,	,,	NE Douai	Albatros DIII	OOC
28.5.17	,,	,,	NE Douai	Albatros DIII	OOC
5.6.17	,,	,,	Fampoux	Albatros DIII	Destroyed
9.6.17	,,	,,	N Douai	Albatros DIII	OOC

* OOC = Downed out of control

ACKNOWLEDGEMENTS

I would like to thank Norman Franks and Hal Giblin for their generosity in supplying information and biographical details on several of the pilots who served with 40 Squadron in 1917.

BIBLIOGRAPHY

Marsden, Barry M., *Winged Warriors*
(Ryestone Publications 2003)

'McScotch' (MacLanachan, William), *Fighter Pilot*
(Greenhill Books 1985)

Shores, Franks and Guest, *Above the Trenches*
(Grub Street 1990)